NEVER BROKEN

HOW GOD REBUILDS WHAT LIFE TRIES TO SHATTER

SYLVESTER JENKINS III

Published by Sylvester Jenkins III
2025 United States

All rights reserved. No part of this book may be reproduced or modified in any form, including photocopying, recording, or by any information storage and retrieval system, without permission in writing from the publisher.

CONTENTS

Acknowledgments	1
PROLOGUE **The Night the Mirror Shattered**	2
INTRODUCTION **The Myth of Brokenness**	4
CHAPTER 1 **The Breaking Point**	11
CHAPTER 2 **Ashes to Beauty**	19
CHAPTER 3 **When the Mask Falls Off**	31
CHAPTER 4 **Carried Through the Cracks**	43
CHAPTER 5 **Built in the Breaking**	53
CHAPTER 6 **The Shift in the Shatter**	63
CHAPTER 7 **Walking in Divine Alignment**	74
CHAPTER 8	

Scars That Speak   83

CHAPTER 9
Becoming Whole   92

CONCLUSION
The Evidence of Purpose   100

A Personal Letter from the Author   110

Pass It On   112

About the Author   113

Small Group Discussion Guide   114

ACKNOWLEDGMENTS

First and foremost, I give all glory and honor to my Lord and Savior, Jesus Christ. Without your grace, guidance, and unfailing love, this message would not exist—nor would I.

To every family member, and friend who prayed for me when I couldn't find the words to pray for myself, thank you. Your intercession carried me through dark nights and helped birth this light.

To my wife and children: Your love, support, and patience have been a shelter in the storm. Thank you for believing in me through every season. You've shown me that strength isn't loud, it's loyal.

To my mentors and spiritual leaders, past and present, who saw something in me even when I was still becoming, thank you for speaking life and direction when I needed it most.

To the readers, those who have wrestled, wept, and walked through seasons of breaking, I wrote this for you. My prayer is that every page reminds you that God is still working, still speaking, and still writing beauty out of the broken places.

This book is a testimony. And testimonies are never created alone.

Thank you.

PROLOGUE

THE NIGHT THE MIRROR SHATTERED

I remember sitting on the edge of a worn mattress in a dimly lit room that felt more like a prison than a place of rest. My elbows were digging into my knees, my face buried in my hands—not in prayer, but in desperation. That night, the silence around me screamed louder than any battlefield I had ever known. I didn't have the strength to fight. I wasn't sure I had the strength to keep going.

I felt like my life had collapsed into pieces, too shattered to put back together. I had lost my mother, my anchor. The grief of that loss cut deeper than words could ever explain. At the same time, my marriage was hanging on by a thread. We were two people in the same house, living in separate storms, drifting further apart with every misunderstood word and missed moment. The man in the mirror was a stranger to me—tired, angry, ashamed, and afraid. I was trying to lead, trying to provide, trying to hold it all together—but inside, I was falling apart.

Maybe you know what it's like to look in the mirror and not recognize the person staring back at you. To feel like you're giving everything, but inside, you're collapsing.

Everything I had worked for—every title, every role—felt like it had slipped through my fingers. I was a soldier, a husband, a father, a leader... but at that moment, I didn't feel like any of those things. I felt lost. Empty. Done. I had carried the weight of pain from childhood, the trauma of the streets in Columbus, Georgia, the scars from battles in uniform, and the silent war of spiritual confusion. And now, it has all caught up with me.

I didn't even know if I believed the words I whispered, but I said them anyway: "God, if You're really real… don't let this be the end of me."

And maybe, just maybe, you're here because you've reached a similar place.

Later that night, something shifted, not in the room, but in me. What looked and felt like the end was actually the beginning. A breaking point became a turning point. I didn't know it then, but I wasn't falling apart, I was being rebuilt.

This book isn't just another story; it's an invitation. An invitation to see your own pain through a different lens. To look at the shattered pieces of your life and discover that you are not broken beyond repair. You are being reshaped for something greater.

INTRODUCTION

THE MYTH OF BROKENNESS

"You were never broken. You were being built, shaped, and positioned for purpose."

For too long, we've let the word "broken" define us. It's become a quiet label, worn like a scarlet letter, a hidden identity we mask with polished smiles and packed schedules. We whisper it when no one's listening: "I'm broken." And we believe it. We carry that belief into our relationships, our dreams, even our prayers. We see the cracks in our lives and mistake them for proof of failure, inadequacy, or unworthiness.

But what if we've misunderstood brokenness altogether?

What if what we were taught to fear is actually the very path God uses to shape us? What if the crushing wasn't meant to destroy, but to prepare? What if you were never broken at all… only being built?

We've Misread the Pain

In both church culture and society, brokenness is often seen as a curse, a flaw that makes you less than, a mark that disqualifies you from being used by God. We talk about restoration as if God plans to glue us back together and pretend the damage never happened. But God doesn't pretend. He's not a God of cover-ups; He's the God of transformation.

There's a vital difference between repair and redemption.

Repair tries to return something to what it used to be. Redemption creates something entirely new from what was lost. God doesn't simply restore us to a former version of ourselves—He transforms us into something more glorious, more refined, more aligned with His purpose.

Pain doesn't mean you're defective. Disappointment doesn't mean you've been discarded. Your wounds do not disqualify you. They are often the sacred places where God's glory shines the brightest. But here's the hard truth: we don't like the process. Because transformation often feels like death before it ever looks like resurrection.

Brokenness Is Not the End—It's The Beginning

If you're reading this and you've experienced betrayal, abandonment, abuse, or failure, you're not alone. The most powerful men and women of God were shaped in seasons of brokenness. Joseph was thrown into a pit and sold by his brothers. David hid in caves, running for his life. Ruth lost everything before stepping into legacy. Jesus was beaten, pierced, and crucified before He was exalted.

So why do we think our stories should be any different?

Why do we believe that God's purpose must come without pain?

We've embraced a Westernized gospel that equates comfort with calling and success with favor. But the truth is, the narrow road, the one that leads to life, is often paved with crushing moments, sleepless nights, unanswered questions, and silent tears. And yet, it's there, in the crucible of pain, that purpose begins to emerge.

You Are Not a Mistake

You need to hear this: you are not a mistake. Your story isn't too messy. Your past isn't too far gone. The broken moments didn't ruin you; they refined you. God knew exactly who you were when He called you. He saw every wound, every regret, every poor choice, every addiction, every loss, and still said, "You're mine. I choose you. I will use even this."

God doesn't call the qualified. He qualifies the called.

He's not looking for perfection, He's looking for willingness.

The Lie of Perfection

Our world idolizes perfection, flawless skin, picture-perfect families, filtered success, and carefully curated highlight reels. We're drowning in a culture that rewards the appearance of wholeness, even when people are falling apart behind closed doors. So we fake it. We smile while grieving. We lead while bleeding. We show up for everyone else, even when we're starving spiritually.

But perfection was never God's requirement. Surrender was.

God isn't moved by polished exteriors. He's moved by broken hearts. Psalm 51:17 says, "The sacrifices of God are a broken spirit; a broken and contrite heart, O God, you will not despise."

Your broken heart is a holy offering. It's not the thing that drives God away; it's what draws Him near.

Reframing The Narrative

It's time to rewrite the narrative. It's time to stop seeing your broken moments as setbacks and start recognizing them as sacred setups. The divorce wasn't the end of your joy. The failure wasn't the end of your future. The pain wasn't the end of your peace. Each one was part of the process—a divine recalibration, aligning you with who you were always meant to be.

This book isn't just about healing. It's about understanding. It's about seeing your life through the lens of God's sovereignty, not your suffering. It's about waking up to the truth that nothing is wasted in His hands.

The Process Hurts, But It's Holy

Let's be honest—the process hurts. There will be moments when it feels like you're losing everything. There will be nights when the weight of disappointment seems unbearable. But you're not being buried. You're being planted.

Seeds must break before they bloom.

Before resurrection, there is crucifixion.

Before the crown, there is always a cross.

You may not see it yet, but every heartbreak, every delay, every loss is doing something within you. It's producing something eternal. Romans 8:18 reminds us, "I consider that our present sufferings are not worth comparing with the glory that will be revealed in us."

There is glory on the other side of this. And you're closer than you think.

You're Still Standing

Maybe you're reading this with tears in your eyes. Maybe you're in the middle of a breaking right now. Maybe everything you've learned has collapsed. If that's you, pause. Breathe. Look around. You're still here.

You're still standing.

Which means the breaking didn't break you.

Yes, it changed you—but not into something worse. It shaped you into someone wiser, stronger, more surrendered, more dependent on God. Someone more filled with grace, grit, and purpose.

A Divine Exchange

The beauty of walking with Jesus is that He never asks us to carry our brokenness alone. He offers an exchange: beauty for ashes, joy for mourning, praise for despair.

He's not afraid of your mess. He's not intimidated by your questions. Your wounds do not repel him. In fact, He draws near to the brokenhearted and binds up the wounds of the crushed (Psalm 34:18).

He meets you in the middle of your brokenness—not to shame you, but to shape you.

What This Book Will Do

This book will not pity you. It won't pacify you. It will push you. It will challenge you to see your life through the eyes of Heaven. It will confront the lies you've believed—about yourself and about God. It will reframe your suffering and give purpose to your past. It will help you rise from the rubble, not just inspired, but transformed.

Each chapter will take you deeper. From the masks you've worn to the wounds you've hidden, from the pain you've buried to the purpose that's been calling your name—you'll begin to see it all through the truth of God's Word and the lens of divine destiny.

This isn't just a book. It's a mirror. A map. A message straight from the heart of God: *You were never broken. You were becoming.*

Please Note:
The stories shared in this book are real, raw, and deeply personal. Some names and identifying details have been changed to protect the privacy of those involved.

These testimonies reflect the heart of Never Broken—that no matter your past, God can rebuild what life tried to shatter. Each journey is sacred, and the courage behind each one offers hope for your own.

Their pain was real. Their healing is powerful. Their names may be changed, but their transformation is true.

Let's Begin Again

So, before you turn the page, I want to leave you with some questions:

What if your greatest pain was actually the birthplace of your greatest purpose?

What if everything that tried to destroy you was actually positioning you for destiny?

What if... You were never broken at all?

Welcome to the beginning of a new narrative.

Welcome to the unveiling of your purpose.

Welcome to *Never Broken*.

> *"You are not being destroyed; you are being deployed. The breaking is heaven's preparation for release."*

CHAPTER 1

THE BREAKING POINT

Key Verse:
"Unless a grain of wheat falls to the ground and dies,
it remains alone; but if it dies, it produces much grain."
– John 12:24

There comes a defining moment in every person's life—what I call the breaking point. It arrives without warning and often without mercy, when everything you've built, everything you've trusted, begins to unravel. It's a season where your faith is shaken, your plans collapse, and what once felt secure comes crashing down. In those moments, it feels like the end, like there's no way forward.

But here's what I've learned—and what I want you to hold on to: in the Kingdom of God, endings are never really endings. They are beginnings in disguise.

In God's economy, the breaking point isn't a sign of failure. It's a sacred threshold that leads us into something greater. God doesn't bring destruction, but He will use disruption. He doesn't set out to break us down, but He will allow the breaking to transform us—to reorient our steps and realign our hearts with His purpose.

In my journey, I can recall several moments when I found myself in what felt like an unending season of hardship. There were times I questioned God, asking, "Why is this happening? Why does it feel like everything is falling apart?" At the time, I couldn't see beyond the pain or the confusion. I had no sense of how this particular season could serve me or lead anywhere better than where I was.

But looking back, I see now that those very moments were the ones that shaped my identity, redefined my purpose, and laid the foundation for the next chapter of my life.

Through those difficult seasons, I've come to understand a profound truth: the breaking point is not the end. It's the beginning of a new level of divine purpose. What feels like destruction is often God's hand clearing away what no longer serves you, so He can position you for what's ahead. The breaking point, though painful, is where you emerge stronger, clearer, and more aligned with the path God has set before you.

What Happens at the Breaking Point?

At the breaking point, everything we once held dear is confronted. We're forced to face the raw, unfiltered truth of our lives—who we are, what we believe, and where we've placed our trust. Breaking reveals the layers of our identity, character, and dependence on things other than God. It's a season of stripping, pruning, and purging. And in that season, we're called to confront what we've hidden from others and ourselves.

Identity Is Confronted

The breaking exposes the difference between who we think we are and who God says we are. It's a hard truth, but a necessary one. In moments of crisis, the things we've built our identity around—our titles, relationships, accomplishments—often fall away. What remains is the raw essence of who we are in Christ. That's where real transformation begins.

For many of us, identity is tied to external things—our jobs, our status, or the approval of others. So when those things are shaken or stripped away, we're left asking, "Who am I now?" But it's in that very moment we begin to understand: our identity isn't in what we do or what we have. It's in who God says we are. In the midst of breaking, God redefines us, reminds us of our worth, and shows us that we are more than our circumstances and more than our achievements.

I remember a time in my life when everything I had worked for seemed to crumble. My marriage shifted, and the very foundation of my world began to fall apart. I share more of that journey in my book From Combat to Comeback, where I open up about moments when I felt lost, unworthy, and ready to give up.

I found myself asking, "Who am I without the success I once achieved?" "Who am I without the relationships that used to define me?" It was in that broken place that I heard God's voice louder than ever before, reminding me that my identity was never tied to my accomplishments or the people around me. My identity was, and always had been, rooted in Christ. And that truth became the anchor I needed to rebuild from the ground up.

Trust Is Tested

When we reach the breaking point, everything that once felt secure can suddenly seem uncertain. We begin to question the very things we used to trust. It's in these moments that our faith is tested. God often strips away every other source of security so we're left with only one thing: our trust in Him. The breaking point isn't punishment—it's divine training. God uses the disruption to teach us how to rely fully on Him, not on our own strength or understanding.

Trust doesn't come easily, especially when everything around us feels like it's falling apart. We're conditioned to trust what we can see and control. But the breaking point pushes us to release those false securities and place our trust in something far greater: God's provision, God's faithfulness, and God's timing.

I remember a time when I had no plan B. The financial stability I had worked so hard to build was suddenly shaken, and I was forced to trust God in a way I never had before. There were no quick answers or easy fixes. All I had was faith that God would come through. And it was in that season of uncertainty that I learned to trust Him with my whole heart, to lean not on my own understanding, and to believe He would make a way, even when I couldn't see one. That experience deepened my trust and taught me this: God is always faithful, even when our circumstances don't reflect our expectations.

Purpose Is Conceived

It's often in the breaking that purpose is conceived. Pain becomes the womb of purpose. Our calling isn't born in comfort; it's born in crisis. God frequently uses the most challenging moments of our lives to birth something greater within us. What once looked like a setback is, in fact, God's setup for something far bigger.

Purpose takes shape in the midst of pain because adversity reveals who we truly are and what we're truly capable of. We're forced to confront our weaknesses, face our fears, and step into our calling in ways we never could have imagined in seasons of ease. The breaking pushes us to dig deeper, to access strength we didn't know we had, and to lean fully on God's power to carry us through.

In my own life, I've learned that my greatest purpose was born from my deepest pain. The losses, the hardships, the struggles, they became the soil where purpose took root. What I once saw as a dead end was actually God preparing the foundation for something new: a greater calling, a deeper impact, and a renewed sense of direction.

God doesn't break what He can't use. He breaks what He's about to multiply.

Everything God allows to be broken, He intends to bless. Just as a seed must break before it bears fruit, purpose must be pressed before it can be released.

The breaking point isn't the end of you, it's the beginning. God breaks who you thought you were to reveal who He created you to be.

Reflection Questions

- **What situation in your life felt like it broke you, but now you see the hand of God in it?**
    - Reflect on a time when you thought your world was falling apart. What can you now see in hindsight that shows God's hand at work in the midst of your pain?

- **Have you been trusting more in your plans than in God's process?**
    - Take a moment to evaluate whether you've been relying on your own understanding and plans more than trusting in God's divine process for your life. What steps can you take to shift your trust back to Him?

- **What has "breaking" taught you about your identity?**
    - Consider how the breaking point has shaped your understanding of who you are in Christ. What false identities or dependencies has God stripped away, and how has that made you more secure in your true identity?

Kingdom Keys:

- **Recognize the Purpose:** Remind yourself that every breaking point is a doorway, not a dead-end.

- **Reflect on Identity:** Regularly revisit who God says you are, not who circumstances have labeled you.
- **Trust God's Timing:** Practice patience by acknowledging God is using current struggles to position you for future purpose.

Personal Reflection Space:

"Identify a recent breaking point in your life. What lesson do you believe God was teaching you at that moment?"

_____

_____

_____

_____

_____

_____

_____

_____

_____

_____

_____

_____

_____

_____

_____

NEVER BROKEN

"You cannot wear a crown of beauty if your hands are still clinging to ashes. Release to receive."

CHAPTER 2

ASHES TO BEAUTY

> *Scripture Focus:*
> *"To all who mourn... He will give a crown of beauty for ashes,*
> *a joyous blessing instead of mourning, festive praise instead of despair."*
> – Isaiah 61:3 (NLT)

There's a divine paradox at the heart of God's Kingdom: what the world sees as ugly, God calls beautiful. What the world casts aside, Heaven gathers and redeems. What looks like ruin to man is often the raw material in the hands of a Creator who sees beyond what we can imagine. This paradox is essential to understanding the beauty of brokenness, a concept often misunderstood, yet deeply powerful when we let it reshape us.

In our world, brokenness is treated as weakness, failure, or irreparable damage. We're taught that when something breaks, it loses its value, its purpose, its potential. But what if that view is not only incomplete, but completely wrong? What if brokenness isn't something to be discarded, but something God uses to create something stronger, richer, and more radiant than before?

Let me clear up the misunderstanding: God alone can take what's broken and make it more powerful, more purposeful, and more beautiful than it ever was. Where the world sees devastation, God sees the potential for transformation. That's the beauty of brokenness, what others call the end, God calls the beginning.

Let me tell you about Tanisha, a young woman who grew up in and out of foster care, burdened by the belief that she was unwanted and unworthy. Her teenage years were marked by self-harm, drug use, and relationships that only deepened her wounds. At 19, she found herself pregnant, alone, living in a motel, and unsure if she could keep the baby.

One cold Sunday, she wandered into a church just to get warm. The message that day came from Isaiah 61:3—beauty for ashes. It hit her like a wave. After the service, a woman from the congregation approached her and invited her to lunch. That simple act became a turning point.

Over the next year, Tanisha joined a small group, gave her life to Christ, and discovered her voice as an advocate for foster youth. Eventually, she became a mentor to teen girls aging out of the system.

The ashes of abandonment became the soil where her purpose took root.

Isaiah's prophecy, beauty for ashes, is more than a poetic promise. It reveals a spiritual truth: God operates through divine exchange. In ancient Jewish tradition, ashes symbolized mourning, loss, and deep grief. People wore ashes when life had broken them, when sorrow weighed heavy and hope felt lost. Ashes were the outward sign of inward despair.

And yet, God promises: "I will give you beauty for your ashes."

This isn't just a comforting thought. It's a sacred transaction. God takes what is broken, what is lost, and transforms it into something full of life, purpose, and beauty.

Ashes Are Evidence

The ashes in your life are not signs of failure; they are proof that something had to die for something greater to be born. Maybe it was a relationship, a dream, your innocence, your confidence, or even a version of yourself that no longer served you. These ashes mark what once was a season where things fell apart, where dreams crumbled, where hope seemed to vanish.

But hear this: God will never ask for your ashes unless He intends to build something new.

Before God raises up something glorious, He often allows certain things to be reduced to ashes. Why? Because what dies in the fire is what cannot serve your future. Some relationships, once close, were burned away because they couldn't walk with you into your next season. Some jobs had to end because they were keeping you from your true calling. Some habits and patterns had to be destroyed because they were stunting your growth, clouding your potential, and distorting your identity.

Ashes mark the end of what was, but beauty marks the beginning of what's to come. In God's hands, your brokenness becomes soil. And from that soil, something new will grow. What looked like the end was actually the start of a process leading you to your greater purpose.

The Process of the Exchange

This exchange —beauty for ashes—is not a wishful thought or an abstract idea. It's a spiritual transaction that requires your active participation. You cannot receive the beauty unless you're willing to bring the ashes. It's a divine principle: to experience the fullness of God's restoration, you must offer Him the remnants of your pain, loss, and disappointment. God never asks for what He isn't prepared to redeem.

Here's the mystery of this exchange: the ashes don't disappear. They're transformed. They don't vanish—they're renewed, reshaped, and elevated for a higher purpose. God wastes nothing. Even your pain carries purpose. Even your brokenness holds value in His hands. What the enemy meant to destroy you with, God will use to elevate you. As Joseph told his brothers, "What the enemy meant for evil, God intended for good" (Genesis 50:20).

Your scars will become your strength. Your wounds will birth your wisdom. Your past mistakes, failures, and regrets will serve as the very platform from which God launches you into your next season. The ashes you carry today are not your burden to bear alone—they are the raw material God will use to build a testimony that leads others to breakthrough.

But here's the key: you must stop clinging to the ashes. Some have built entire homes in places they were only meant to pass through. They've made mourning their permanent address. They rehearse the pain, wear the ashes like a badge, and live in a constant state of grief. But God is calling you to release the ashes, to let go of the pain so He can redeem it and exchange it for purpose.

If you're ready to move forward, God is ready to transform your ashes into something beautiful.

Lessons From the Potter

One of the most beautiful images of God's work in our lives is found in the story of the potter and the clay in Jeremiah 18. God told the prophet to go to the potter's house, and there he saw the potter working at the wheel, shaping the clay. The vessel was marred, broken and misshapen—but the potter didn't throw it away. Instead, he reshaped it into another vessel, one that seemed good to him.

This is the heart of how God works in us. Even when we are bruised, scarred, or broken by life, He does not discard us. He reshapes us. The breaking is never to destroy us—it is to transform us into something greater. The potter never abandoned the clay, and God will never abandon you. No matter how shattered you feel, you are still in His hands. And in those hands, you are being remade according to a vision you may not yet fully see—but one He is crafting with divine precision.

The potter's work is never rushed. He shapes with care, with patience, and with love. And just like that, Clay, we are always in process. The breaking is necessary because it is through the breaking that we are reformed and prepared for the future God has already designed for us.

Your Beauty Has Purpose

When God gives beauty for ashes, it's not just about making you feel better—it's about equipping you to walk in purpose. Healing is not the final destination; assignment is. God doesn't simply heal us to make us whole; He heals us so we can become vessels of healing for others.

Once you've received beauty for your brokenness, you become an agent of transformation in the lives of others. You are no longer just a recipient of grace—you're a conduit through which His grace flows. Your testimony becomes a key that unlocks someone else's healing. Your redemption isn't only for you; it's preparation to help others find their way to freedom.

Revelation 12:11 tells us, "They have defeated him by the blood of the Lamb and the word of their testimony." Your testimony is more than a story about past struggles—it's a roadmap to freedom for someone else. The beauty God gave you isn't meant to be hoarded. It's meant to be shared. Once redeemed, your brokenness becomes a powerful tool through which others are set free.

I'll never forget the first time I shared my full testimony publicly. It wasn't behind a pulpit or under bright stage lights. It was in a small, dimly lit room filled with men who, like me, had wrestled with failure, shame, and hopelessness. Some were just beginning to gather the broken pieces of their lives. Others weren't sure they even had the strength to try. I saw it in their faces—the same emptiness I once carried, the same silence that used to sit heavy on my spirit.

I was nervous. I had spent so long trying to move past my past that revisiting it felt overwhelming. But in that moment, God whispered to my heart: "Your freedom isn't just for you. It's for them, too."

So, with trembling hands and an obedient heart, I told my story. I spoke of the childhood trauma. The streets that nearly swallowed me. The inner battles no one could see. I shared the failures, the regrets, the nights I questioned my worth and purpose. I spoke about the day I almost gave up completely—and the moment God stepped in.

As I spoke, something shifted in the room. Walls came down. I saw it in their eyes. Men hardened by life began to soften. Some wiped away tears they hadn't allowed to fall in years. Others nodded silently, as if hearing their own hidden pain spoken aloud for the first time.

When I finished, there was no applause. No grand celebration. Just a sacred silence—and then a line began to form. One by one, they came forward. Some asked for prayer. Some asked for hope. And some simply said, "If God could do it for you, maybe He can do it for me, too."

That night, dozens of men gave their lives to Christ—not because I preached a polished sermon, but because I dared to tell the truth about my brokenness. That's when I realized: the enemy doesn't just fear your healing—he fears your testimony. He fears what happens when you stop hiding your scars and start using them to light the way for others.

Since that night, God has opened doors for me to share my story across churches, prisons, recovery centers, and leadership events. Every time I speak, I'm reminded that our greatest weapon isn't perfection—it's redemption. It's the raw, unfiltered account of how God met us in the ashes and made something beautiful out of what was once broken.

And I've seen miracles unfold. I've watched hardened hearts soften. I've seen men who thought they were too far gone crumble under the weight of grace. I've witnessed women step into healing after carrying shame for decades—all because someone dared to be real. I've seen young people teetering on the edge of despair rediscover purpose simply because they heard that if God could use someone like me, then maybe—just maybe—He could use someone like them.

You see, when you share your testimony, you're not just remembering the past—you're releasing a prophecy. You're declaring that the same God who rescued, redeemed, and restored you can—and will—do the same for anyone who calls on His name.

Your testimony breaks chains. It silences shame. It shifts atmospheres and ignites faith in those who've forgotten how to believe. It builds bridges over the chasms created by pain and pride. It's your weapon against the lies of the enemy—and one of the most powerful gifts you can offer a broken world.

You are the evidence that God still redeems, still restores, still resurrects.

The world doesn't need another polished performance or filtered presentation. It needs real testimonies of real grace. People need to know that God still meets us in the rubble. He still brings beauty from ashes. He still writes redemption stories using broken pens and shattered pieces.

You are that story.

So never underestimate the power of your testimony. Never downplay the process God brought you through. Because someone's future might hinge on your willingness to say, "If He did it for me, He can do it for you."

The Mindset Shift: From Shame to Sacred

False Narrative #1: "My pain disqualifies me."
Mindset Shift: My pain is evidence of my preparation.

God doesn't need you to have it all together. In fact, your brokenness is often the very thing He uses to birth a new purpose. Redemption doesn't deny pain—it transforms it.

False Narrative #2: "If I had more faith, this wouldn't have happened."
Mindset Shift: Faith is not about avoiding fire—it's trusting God in the middle of it.
Jesus didn't say, "If you believe, you'll never have trials." He said, "In this world, you will have trouble. But take heart—I've overcome it." (*John 16:33*)

False Narrative #3: "If it ended, I failed."
Mindset Shift: *Sometimes God allows things to end because they can't carry the weight of your calling.*
That friendship, that job, that version of you—it may have been necessary for a season, but not every assignment is forever. God brings things to a close not to hurt you, but to release you into something greater.

What I've learned is that every toxic thought we hold onto has a real, physical effect on our brain. But the opposite is also true: when we reframe painful memories through the lens of purpose and hope, new, healthy neural pathways begin to form.

When you trade your ashes for beauty, you're not just making a spiritual exchange—you're rewiring your mind. Gratitude, faith, and a focused trust in God's promises activate your brain's ability to heal. Restoration happens not just in your spirit, but deep within your being.

Kingdom Keys:

- **Exchange Your Ashes:** Daily surrender your disappointments and struggles in prayer to receive God's beauty.
- **Stop Rehearsing Pain:** Intentionally replace painful memories with reminders of God's promises.

- **Recognize Divine Opportunities:** View setbacks as setups for something new that God wants to do in your life.

Reflection Questions

- **What ashes are you still holding onto—grief, regret, offense, failure?**
  - Take a moment to reflect on the things you've been holding onto. Are there areas in your life where you've allowed pain and loss to define you? Are you ready to release them to God?
- **Can you see any beauty God has already brought from past pain?**
  - Think about your past struggles. Have you been able to see how God has already transformed some of your pain into purpose?
- **Are you ready to stop rehearsing the pain and start releasing it for purpose?**
  - Are you ready to let go of the cycle of rehearing your pain and instead begin to see it as a catalyst for growth and healing in your life and the lives of others?

Declaration Prayer

Father, I thank You that You do not waste my pain. I offer you every broken piece, every loss, every disappointment. I lay my ashes at Your feet. Exchange them for beauty. Give me vision where there was once despair, hope where there was once mourning. I trust that you are making something beautiful out of my story. In Jesus' name, Amen.

Personal Reflection Space:

"List one specific 'ash' from your past that you're ready to exchange for God's beauty. Why is this important for your growth?"

_____

_____

> *"Authenticity isn't weakness, it's biological warfare against anxiety and emotional fragmentation."*

CHAPTER 3

WHEN THE MASK FALLS OFF

Scripture Focus:
"And we all, who with unveiled faces contemplate the Lord's glory, are being transformed into His image..."
– 2 Corinthians 3:18 (NIV)

Across cultures, masks have long been used to conceal what lies beneath—whether for celebration, protection, or performance. But here's the truth: while masks may shield us in the short term, they hinder transformation in the long run. You cannot be healed while pretending to be whole. You cannot walk in freedom while performing for approval.

The Kingdom of God moves in the opposite direction from the world. Where the world encourages hiding, God invites unveiling.

There comes a moment in every believer's journey when God lovingly confronts the mask, not to shame you, but to reveal who you truly are underneath. That moment is sacred. It's where true identity is rediscovered, and where divine transformation begins.

Let me say this plainly: God can only anoint the real you, not the version you present to impress others, not the one curated to gain approval, but the you He created and already knows.

The Purpose of the Mask

The mask we wear has one purpose: protection. Protection from judgment. Protection from rejection. Protection from failure. Protection from admitting that we don't have it all together. From an early age, we learn how to put on these masks. We wear them to shield ourselves from the world, and over time, they harden into false identities. What begins as a defense becomes a prison, locking us away from the fullness of our God-given identity.

But here's the tragedy: some people die never having lived as their true selves. They live and die as who others expect them to be. They never taste the freedom of authenticity. They never know the joy of being fully known—without pretense, without hiding, without fear. In the Kingdom of God, freedom begins where pretending ends.

The masks may win us temporary applause, but they come at a cost. They rob us of intimacy. They erode true connection. And most painfully, they obscure our purpose. You cannot fulfill your calling while wearing a costume. Your calling is too sacred, too weighty, too vital to be constrained by the illusion of who you think you should be.

I learned this the hard way.

There was a season when, from the outside, my life looked like a picture of success. A thriving career. Public recognition. Leadership influence. A loving family. I had what people said I should want. But inside, I was suffocating. I had built my identity on strength, achievement, and always having the answers. Admitting weakness felt like betrayal—not just of others' expectations, but of the persona I had carefully constructed.

Then came a moment I'll never forget.

It was a quiet evening. I was alone in the living room after everyone had gone to bed. The house was still and dimly lit, just the soft glow of a single lamp casting shadows on the walls. I sat there, shoulders slumped, heart heavy. And for the first time in a long time, I let the truth escape my lips in a whisper:

"I'm tired of pretending."

I realized that night that the mask I had worn for so long—the mask of "I'm fine," the mask of "I've got it all under control"—had become too heavy to carry. I had spent so much of my life performing for the approval of others that I no longer knew what it felt like to simply be. To breathe without measuring myself against invisible standards. To speak without fear of being misunderstood. To fail without believing I was a failure.

In the quiet of that room, God met me—not the version I tried to present to the world, but the real me. The broken, tired, scared me. And he didn't scold me for being weak. He didn't ask me to pull myself together. Instead, He reminded me that He loved me, not the polished image, not the public persona, but the raw, unfinished, messy version I tried to hide.

Tears streamed down my face as the weight of years of performance began to lift. That moment marked the beginning of a new journey—a journey toward authenticity. A journey I'm still walking. One that continues to teach me this truth: God cannot bless who you pretend to be. He can only bless who you really are.

Maybe you've worn masks too. Maybe you've believed the lie that if you ever showed your real struggles, your real fears, your real doubts, you'd be rejected. But hear me, freedom is not found in hiding. Freedom is found in unveiling.

That season didn't just expose my pain; it forged my disciplines. It was through my unraveling that I began to build habits that anchored me beyond the applause and activity.

1. **The Discipline of Stillness**
   Psalm 46:10 says, "Be still and know that I am God." I had mistaken motion for momentum. In the stillness, I began to hear God again—not in the noise of my busyness, but in the quiet of His presence. I started carving out time in my day to do nothing but sit before Him. No agenda. No preaching prep. No fixing. Just being.

2. **The Practice of Honest Journaling**
   For too long, I had filtered my prayers like I filtered my posts—polished and packaged. But I began to journal raw prayers. Not sanitized ones. Honest ones. I told God about my anger, my fears, my confusion. And in those pages, I found His voice. Not in judgment—but in healing.

3. **Choosing Obedience Over Image**
   I stopped chasing what looked good and started pursuing what was good for me. I left positions that fed my pride but starved my soul. I began saying no more often—to invitations, opportunities, and expectations that didn't align with my health or assignment.

Adam, Where Are You?

After Adam and Eve sinned, they did two things: they hid, and they covered themselves. God, who had walked with them in the cool of the garden, came looking. He asked a question He already knew the answer to: "Adam, where are you?"

This wasn't about geography. It was about identity. "Where is the real you, Adam? The one I created in my image? The one who walked with Me—uncovered, unashamed, unafraid?"

Sin doesn't just separate us from God—it convinces us we must hide from Him. It brings shame. It tells us that if anyone saw the real us, they'd turn away.

But here's the beautiful truth: God already sees you. He sees the parts of you you've tried to hide—the parts that feel unworthy, broken, ashamed. And still, He comes looking. He doesn't run from your vulnerability. He meets you in it. Not to condemn you, but to call you back to who you really are.

The Danger of Performance Christianity

We live in a society that idolizes performance. We've mastered the art of smiling when we're hurting, speaking in spiritual clichés when we feel lost, and dressing the part while feeling empty inside. We know how to play the role, serve faithfully, and say all the right things—even while our hearts are quietly breaking.

But here's the truth: God is not impressed by performance. He's not moved by our ability to act. He's not looking for actors—He's looking for sons and daughters. The Kingdom of God is not a stage; it's a family.

Performance Christianity is exhausting. It traps you in a cycle of striving, pretending, and fearing exposure. But when you live from your identity in Christ, you stop performing for approval. You begin to live from a place of rest, not striving. You know who you are. You know who you are.

When you live from your identity as God's beloved, you no longer have to prove yourself. You are free to be exactly who He created you to be—without pretending, without hiding. And in that freedom, real transformation begins.

You Cannot Heal What You Hide

It's a difficult truth, but a necessary one: God cannot fix what you fake. Healing begins the moment the mask comes off. Sometimes the most powerful act of spiritual warfare isn't slaying giants or casting out demons—it's choosing to be honest. To be real.

James 5:16 says, "Confess your faults one to another, and pray for one another, that you may be healed." It doesn't say, hide your faults or cover your weaknesses. It says confess. Healing flows from honesty.

Transparency is the currency of transformation. You don't need to broadcast your pain to everyone, but you do need to be real with God and with the trusted people He's placed in your life. Vulnerability isn't weakness. It's a strength. It opens the door to healing, growth, and genuine connection.

Here's the truth: **An enemy exposed is an enemy defeated.**
You are only as strong as your biggest secret. The enemy of your soul thrives in darkness. He whispers lies in hidden places and gains power in your silence. But the moment you bring that hidden thing into the light, the enemy loses his grip. Darkness cannot overpower the light of truth.

When I was in the Army, one of the things we were trained to do was to identify the enemy, to locate their position, recognize their tactics, and anticipate their next move. Why? Because you can't win a war against a threat you pretend isn't there.
We ran drills, studied maps, and trained relentlessly, not because we liked the fight, but because we knew our lives depended on it.

The same applies in spiritual warfare. If you won't face your wounds, or your secret sin, you give the enemy territory in your life. But when you expose the enemy, when you name it, confess what's been hiding in your heart, you take back ground.

Who Are You Without the Titles?

One of the most deceptive masks we wear is the mask of titles. Pastor. Leader. Entrepreneur. Husband. Wife. Soldier. These are roles, but they are not your identity. The danger comes when we confuse what we do with who we are. And when the role shifts or is stripped away, we're left asking, "Who am I now?"

Here's the truth: you are not what you do. You are who God says you are. Titles can be lost in an instant. But sonship is eternal. Your identity in Christ is the only one that cannot be shaken.

Jesus modeled this perfectly. He never performed for approval. He wasn't swayed by opinions or titles. He lived from a deep, abiding relationship with the Father. His confidence came not from His role, but from His identity.

Jesus Wore No Mask

Jesus was the most authentic person to ever walk the earth. He never once wore a religious mask to gain approval. He didn't pretend to be who others wanted Him to be. He didn't soften His message to please the crowd. He lived fully and unapologetically as Himself—and that's why He could confidently say, "I only do what I see the Father doing" (John 5:19).

Jesus didn't perform for applause. He didn't seek validation from others. He operated in the fullness of His purpose because He knew who He was and Whose He was. He lived from the Father's approval, not for man's.

And when you know who you are in God, you no longer need outside affirmation to feel worthy. You don't need to wear a mask to feel accepted. You can stand in the truth of who you are, and that kind of authenticity is what changes the world.

The Power of Vulnerability

In our culture, vulnerability is often mistaken for weakness. But in the Kingdom of God, it's a source of strength. Vulnerability is not a liability—it's a doorway to connection, healing, and transformation.

Jesus wept. He grew tired. He asked His disciples to stay and pray with Him in His darkest hour. If the Son of God could be vulnerable, why do we think we have to hide our own weaknesses?

Vulnerability is what connects us. It allows others to walk with us on the journey of healing. When you allow yourself to be seen, you give others permission to take off their masks, too.

Transformation doesn't happen through hype—it happens through honesty. Revival begins where authenticity, transparency, and connection are present.

Let me tell you about a close friend of mine, David. He's the executive pastor of a thriving church. He preached powerfully, led with charisma, and checked all the ministry boxes. But behind closed doors, he wrestled with severe anxiety and panic attacks. For years, he wore the mask of spiritual strength, terrified that if anyone knew, he'd be disqualified.

One Sunday morning, in the middle of service, David collapsed. The doctors diagnosed it as a stress-induced breakdown. Lying in that hospital bed, he heard the Holy Spirit whisper, "You've been serving Me with a mask on. I want the real you."

David took a sabbatical, got into therapy, and began a journey of healing. Eventually, he stood before his congregation not as a polished preacher, but as a broken, honest man. He shared his struggle with raw vulnerability.

What followed was a culture shift. Others in his church began opening up. People found permission to stop pretending. They sought help. Healing began.

His ministry didn't shrink. It grew because people finally saw a pastor who wasn't performing, just pursuing grace.

Authenticity Heals the Brain

Science now supports what Scripture has long taught. Hiding your pain keeps your body in survival mode. It raises cortisol levels and places your brain in a chronic state of stress. But when you practice vulnerability—

through confession, transparency, and acceptance—your body releases oxytocin and serotonin, chemicals that promote healing, calm, and connection.

The moment you remove the mask, your mind shifts from defense to restoration. You're not just taking off a social disguise—you're aligning your body and spirit with the truth. And in that alignment, healing begins.

Kingdom Keys

- **Ask God to reveal your true identity.**
    - Spend time in His presence, in His Word. Let Him remind you of who you really are.

- **Find safe spaces for confession and connection.**
    - Healing often happens in a community. Find trusted people who can walk with you as you take off the mask.

- **Live from sonship, not performance.**
    - Your worth is not defined by your actions; it is defined by who God says you are.

- **Celebrate authenticity in others.**
    - Create a culture where realness is honored and vulnerability is embraced.

Reflection Questions

- **What mask have you been wearing out of fear or insecurity?**
    - Reflect on the roles or facades you've created to hide your true self. What are you afraid people will see if you remove your mask?

- **In what ways has performance replaced intimacy with God in your life?**
  - Consider the times you've tried to impress God or others with your actions rather than simply being honest with Him.

- **Are you willing to be seen as you really are, so God can use you as you were truly created?**
  - Are you ready to embrace your true identity in Christ, without the need for pretense or performance?

Declaration Prayer

Father, I come before You without pretense. No more masks. No more pretending. I surrender every false identity I've worn and ask You to reveal the truth of who I am in You. Help me to live from a place of sonship, not striving. Heal every place I've hidden out of fear. Let your love make me whole and real. In Jesus' name, Amen.

Personal Reflection Space:

"Write down one mask you're ready to let go of and why:"

_____

_____

_____

_____

_____

_____

_____

_____

> "Sometimes, the greatest miracles aren't found in unbroken strength but in the grace that carries us through the cracks."

CHAPTER 4

CARRIED THROUGH THE CRACKS

Scripture Focus:
"The Lord is close to the brokenhearted and saves those who are crushed in spirit."
– Psalm 34:18 (NIV)

In the lives of those who feel as though they are falling apart, a quiet miracle is unfolding: God is carrying them through the cracks. When everything seems to be crumbling—when your strength is gone and your hope feels like it's slipping away—it may feel like you're losing everything. But in truth, you are being held together by invisible hands.

The cracks in your life are not signs of failure; they are the very places where God's grace shines brightest.

Let me remind you of something powerful: just because you feel broken doesn't mean you've been abandoned. Just because your situation is cracked doesn't mean your purpose is compromised. In fact, it's often in our most fragile moments that God does His most faithful work.

The cracks are not evidence of God's absence—they are proof of His presence. They are the spaces where His love seeps in, where His strength upholds you, and where His grace sustains you.

You may not be able to see it yet, but He is carrying you through the brokenness, holding you together in ways you cannot fully grasp. And even now, in the midst of it all, He is preparing you for something greater.

The Myth of Holding It Together

In our culture, strength is often defined by the ability to hold everything together. We're taught that true strength comes from staying in control—keeping all the pieces in place, no matter the cost. But in the Kingdom of God, strength is not about control. It's about surrender. It's not about hiding our cracks; it's about letting God work through them.

Too often, believers live under the burden of being the "strong one"—the one who never shows weakness, never sheds a tear, never admits to struggling. But here's the truth: God isn't impressed by your performance of strength. He's drawn to your dependence on His strength. Real strength isn't the absence of weakness; it's the courage to acknowledge it and trust God to carry you through it.

Even Jesus, in His humanity, leaned on the Father during His breaking moment. In the Garden of Gethsemane, He said, "My soul is overwhelmed with sorrow to the point of death" (Matthew 26:38). If Jesus "the Son of God" needed divine support, what makes us think we don't?

Jesus didn't hold it all together through willpower. He surrendered. And in that surrender, He encountered the sustaining power of God's grace.

Grace in the Gaps

The apostle Paul understood what it meant to be carried through the cracks. In 2 Corinthians 12, he speaks of a "thorn in the flesh"—a persistent pain, a weakness that seemed out of place in the life of a spiritual leader. He pleaded with God to take it away, but instead, God responded with these life-altering words: "My grace is sufficient for you, for My power is made perfect in weakness" (2 Corinthians 12:9).

God didn't remove the thorn—He carried Paul through it. This is the mystery of grace: it fills the gaps. It sustains us when our strength gives out. It covers us when life exposes us. Grace doesn't just patch the cracks; it moves through them, making us whole in a way only God can.

God may not eliminate every weakness or hardship, but He will never let you fall through them. His grace is the glue, the net, the lifeline—holding you steady even when everything else feels like it's falling apart. When you feel like you're breaking, God is already at work, weaving grace into every fracture. The cracks aren't where you fail—they're where His grace flows in.

The Cracked Vessel Still Pours

In ancient times, cracked vessels were often discarded, deemed useless and unworthy. But in God's Kingdom, the cracked vessel isn't thrown away—it's chosen. It's through these very cracks that God's glory shines the brightest. The apostle Paul described our bodies as "jars of clay" that carry a treasure—the very presence and power of God (2 Corinthians 4:7).

Your cracks don't disqualify you—they qualify you. The places where you feel the weakest, the most broken, are the very places where God's strength is made perfect. If your life feels cracked, it might be because glory is trying to break through. God receives glory from your survival. He's glorified when others see that you're still standing, even after what should have crushed you. When people look at your life and say, "I don't know how they made it," that's when you know you're being carried by something greater than yourself.

I once met a remarkable woman named Evelyn. At 57, she was diagnosed with early-onset Alzheimer's, just a year after her husband passed unexpectedly. She had been a worship leader, a counselor, and the spiritual anchor of her family. As her memory began to fade, she battled shame and a deep sense of uselessness.

But her daughter noticed something miraculous: even when Evelyn forgot names or how to cook, she could still sing worship songs, word for word.

One day, during a moment of clarity, Evelyn looked at her granddaughter and said, "I may not remember everything, but I know who carries me. Jesus won't forget me, even if I forget myself."

That simple sentence became a sacred declaration in their home. Evelyn's presence—though cracked—remained holy. Her life became a daily testimony of grace, filling the gaps.

Even in decline, she was a vessel of peace. Her family learned to see God in the broken rhythms of her journey.

Just like Evelyn, your cracks are not signs of failure. They are the very places where God is working, pouring His strength and His glory through you. Your brokenness becomes the window through which others witness the power, grace, and sustaining love of God.

God Carries What You Can't

One of the greatest revelations you can ever experience is this: God is not asking you to carry what He already paid for. Isaiah 53:4 declares, "Surely He has borne our griefs and carried our sorrows." If God has already carried your burdens, then why are you still holding onto them?

Many of us are emotionally exhausted, spiritually drained, and mentally overwhelmed—not because life is too heavy, but because we're carrying things we were never meant to bear. We carry grief. We carry fear. We carry trauma, pressure, and unmet expectations. And all of it weighs us down. But God is whispering, "Lay it down. Let me carry it for you."

He's not just offering relief—He's offering rest. He's saying, "Let me carry the pressure, the heartbreak, the shame, the fear. Let me carry you."

You were never designed to shoulder the full weight of life. You were created to walk with the One who bears it on your behalf. And when you release—when you truly trust Him to carry what you cannot—you'll find a peace that surpasses all understanding. You'll discover rest in the midst of your struggle. You'll come to know that you are not alone in the cracks—you are being held together by the hands of the One who created the stars.

The Ministry of "Just Enough"

Have you ever noticed that during your darkest moments, things didn't always get better immediately, but somehow, you had just enough strength to keep going? That's the ministry of God's grace. He may not change your circumstances overnight, but He gives you just enough for the moment. Just enough peace to rest. Just enough clarity to take the next step. Just enough joy to keep believing.

I'll never forget a season in my life when I was walking through one of the darkest valleys I had ever faced. My mind was clouded with fear. My finances were tighter than a clenched fist in a fight for survival. I remember sitting at the kitchen table, staring at a stack of unpaid bills and a heart full of questions. I didn't have the answers. I didn't have the resources. All I had was a flicker of faith that refused to go out completely.

There were nights I lay awake, staring at the ceiling, just trying to find the will to face another day. I wasn't even asking for a miracle—I was just asking for strength. And somehow, day after day, God provided. Not always in the way I asked. Not always in the way I hoped. But every day, He gave me enough. Enough courage to show up again. Enough hope to keep breathing. Enough provision to keep the lights on, the car running, and the family fed.

That "just enough" season is sacred. It teaches you how to rely on God in ways that comfort never could. It strips away illusions of control and self-sufficiency. It pushes you straight into the arms of the One who never runs out. It builds muscles you didn't know you had—faith muscles, endurance muscles, trust muscles.

At the time, I thought I was barely surviving. But looking back now, I realize God was strengthening me. Purifying me. Preparing me. The cracks I saw forming weren't signs of collapse—they were the places where His grace was pouring in. His strength was made perfect in my weakness. His love was holding me together when everything else seemed to fall apart.

One day, when you look back on your own "just enough" season, you'll recognize something powerful: You didn't carry yourself through it—God carried you. Every sleepless night, every whispered prayer, every anxious morning—grace was there. Mercy was there. Provision was there. God Himself was there, in the middle of the mess, quietly working all things for your good.

The cracks you feared were evidence of failure were actually proof of God's faithfulness. That "just enough" wasn't meant to shame you—it was meant to shape you. It was God's reminder that your survival never depended on your own strength—it always depended on Him. And he has never failed you yet.

Kingdom Keys

- **Stop pretending you're not cracked.**
    - Be honest with God and with yourself. God doesn't bless your false image—He blesses your surrender. Let Him into your brokenness.

- **Invite God into the cracks.**
    - Don't hide your pain from God. Present it to Him in prayer, and let Him fill your cracks with His grace and healing.

- **Refuse to measure progress by appearance.**
  - Don't look at your life based on external success. God may be doing more in your weakness than you can see in your strength.

- **Let others help carry you.**
  - Moses needed Aaron and Hur. Jesus needed His disciples. You're not less spiritual for needing support; you're more human. Lean on the community God has placed around you.

Reflection Questions

- **What cracks have you been trying to cover instead of letting God carry?**
  - Reflect on the areas in your life where you've been hiding your weaknesses or pain. Are you ready to let God carry those cracks for you?

- **In what ways has God sustained you, even when you felt like you were falling apart?**
  - Think about the moments when you felt overwhelmed but somehow found the strength to keep going. How did God sustain you in those moments?

- **Are you willing to release the pressure and let God carry what's too heavy for you?**
  - Are you ready to let go of the burdens you've been carrying and trust God to carry them for you?

Declaration Prayer

Father, I confess that I feel cracked in places I can't fix. But I thank You that Your grace carries me through every gap. You are near to the brokenhearted, and I am not alone. I release every weight, every pressure, and every unspoken burden into Your hands. I will not pretend to be whole—I will be honest and let you be my strength. In You, I am not falling apart—I am being held together. In Jesus' name, Amen.

Personal Reflection Space:

"What hidden cracks are now becoming the very places God is using to pour out His grace?"

_____
_____
_____
_____
_____
_____
_____
_____
_____
_____
_____
_____
_____
_____
_____
_____

NEVER BROKEN

"If God is breaking you, it's because He's building something eternal. You are not a project— you are a vessel of purpose."

CHAPTER 5

BUILT IN THE BREAKING

Scripture Focus:
"But He knows the way that I take; when He has tested me,
I will come forth as gold."
– Job 23:10 (NIV)

In the Kingdom of God, there is a profound truth we must embrace: pain has purpose. The world teaches us to avoid pain—to see it as a flaw, a failure, or a detour from the life we should be living. But in God's hands, pain is never pointless. Nothing is wasted—not your wounds, not your tears, not even your scars. God uses what hurts to shape what heals. He allows the breaking not to destroy you, but to develop you.

Every crack, every tear, every scar is part of your becoming. It all works together in the quiet construction of transformation. The fire you're walking through is not for your ruin—it's for your refinement. Like gold tested in the fire, your faith, your character, and your calling are being purified.

This is a hard truth to accept, but one we must grow into: the breaking doesn't mean you're failing—it means you're forming. Just because it hurts doesn't mean God has left you. It may be the very evidence that He is at work within you. The breaking is the tool. The pain is the chisel. The tears are the water softening the clay.

God is building something stronger. Something wiser. Something more aligned with His original purpose for you. You are not falling apart—you are being rebuilt. And when this season has passed, you will come forth not as the same person, but as gold—refined, radiant, and ready.

Wounds That Build

When we think of being "built," we often imagine smooth progress, step-by-step success, and visible victories. But God doesn't build like man builds. His methods are different. His blueprint includes breaking.

Think about Jesus. Before He was crowned the resurrected King, He was first the broken Lamb. His body was pierced, His soul anguished, His back torn open. And yet, through His wounds, we were healed (Isaiah 53:5). His breaking wasn't a sign of weakness—it was the foundation of redemption. His pain became our path to restoration.

Likewise, your wounds—your heartbreak, rejections, disappointments, and betrayals—are not meaningless. They are not random. They are the sacred bricks in the foundation God is laying beneath your calling. The very things you thought would break you are the materials God is using to build you.

God doesn't allow pain just for the sake of suffering. He allows it because He's building something eternal in you. Every wound becomes a part of the structure He is crafting to carry His presence. These aren't marks of failure. They are evidence of formation. They're not signs of defeat; they are symbols of divine design.

You may not see it now, but when God finishes the work, you'll realize: the breaking wasn't the end—it was the beginning of something unshakable.

Pain Builds Capacity

In the Kingdom, pain is never pointless. It doesn't just break us—it stretches us. It digs deep beneath the surface and expands our capacity to carry the weight of the calling God has placed on our lives. Pain doesn't merely wound—it reveals. It exposes the weaknesses we've hidden or ignored, and in that exposure, God begins His work of reinforcement. Where we are weak, He pours in strength.

Job, amidst unspeakable suffering, declared, "He knows the way that I take; when He has tested me, I will come forth as gold" (Job 23:10). The testing was brutal. The refining fire was fierce. But Job knew—this wasn't the end. It was the process of transformation. He didn't emerge from the storm the same man who walked into it. He came out refined, proven, and stronger than before.

You are not being broken to remain in pieces. You are being refined for a purpose, shaped for a calling, and prepared for a weight of glory greater than anything you've carried before. God is far more concerned with who you become in the fire than how quickly you come out of it. Because he's not just delivering you, He's developing you.

He's building in you the character, the endurance, and the wisdom needed to walk confidently in the purpose He's ordained for you. This pain is not your end, it's your preparation.

From Crushed to Commissioned

Let's return to the image of the olive. An olive cannot produce oil until it is crushed. It must be pressed before it can pour. The oil—the anointing—doesn't flow until there's pressure. In the same way, the anointing on your life is often unlocked through seasons of crushing. The breaking you endure is not a sign of abandonment—it's a sign that something powerful is about to be released.

Consider David. He was anointed as king while still a shepherd, chosen in secret while the world still saw a boy. But before he ever sat on the throne, he went through years of caves, betrayal, isolation, and battle. Why? Because the breaking built the king. His leadership, his worship, his heart after God—these were not born on a throne but forged in the fire of hardship.

If David had skipped the process, he would've been ill-prepared for the palace. If you skip the breaking, you sabotage the building. God will never elevate what hasn't been refined. He's not interested in rushing your rise—He's interested in strengthening your foundation.

So if you find yourself in a season of pressure—pressed but not crushed, stretched but not broken—don't resist it. Lean in. Let it do its work. Because the pressure isn't there to destroy you—it's there to release the oil. It's preparing you, shaping you, and equipping you for the calling ahead.

You're not being crushed to be discarded. You're being crushed to be poured out.

Character Is Forged in the Fire

Talent may open the door, but it's character that determines how long you stay in the room. And character isn't built in moments of ease—it's forged in the crucible of hardship.

God is far more concerned with your character than your comfort. He loves you too much to let you stay shallow, so He allows the heat of adversity to burn away pride, expose insecurity, and anchor your identity in Him. This isn't punishment—it's preparation.

Look at Joseph. His gift of interpreting dreams remained constant, but it was the prison that shaped the humility and integrity needed to govern a nation. Moses had the heart of a leader, but it was the wilderness that refined his patience, crushed his impulsiveness, and taught him how to walk with God. Even Jesus, full of divine authority, endured 40 days in the desert before stepping into public ministry. Why? Because testing precedes promotion. Formation comes before elevation.

God is not nearly as impressed with what you can do as He is invested in who you are becoming. The fire you're walking through is not meant to destroy you—it's shaping the kind of character that can carry the weight of your calling.

So, don't despise the process. You're not being punished. You're being prepared.

You Are the Temple He's Building

Paul reminds us in 1 Corinthians 6:19 that our bodies are temples of the Holy Spirit. That means your life is a sacred space, and God is building that space with great intention. He doesn't build anything halfway. He lays the foundation, clears the debris, and constructs with precision and purpose.

But here's the truth: before any construction begins, there must be demolition. God has to tear down what doesn't belong so He can establish what does. If he's stripping things away—relationships, opportunities, desires—it's not rejection. It's a renovation. It's not cruelty. It's construction. He's preparing you to carry His glory.

Sometimes what you think is essential is only temporary scaffolding. When God removes it, He's not leaving you empty—He's making room for something eternal. Trust the demolition. Because what feels like breaking is really clearing the ground for a breakthrough.

I'll never forget meeting Javonte during prison ministry. He grew up in a violent neighborhood in Memphis. By 16, he was deep in gang life—addiction, retaliation, chaos. At 21, he was arrested after a robbery went wrong. While awaiting trial, I handed him a Bible and simply said, "God still has a plan for you."

He scoffed—but he kept the Bible.

Night after night, he read it. When he reached the story of Joseph—betrayed, imprisoned, yet still chosen—something shifted. In that cell, Javonte surrendered his life to Christ. He enrolled in seminary courses, got clean, and began ministering to other inmates.

After his release, he became a reentry counselor and speaker. What once broke him became the foundation God used to build a new legacy—restoring families, saving lives, and showing others that redemption is real.

In the Kingdom, greatness always comes through process. Potential is activated through pressure. And your breaking is not a sign of weakness—it's the birthplace of dominion.

What God is building in you cannot be formed without the fire.

Kingdom Keys to Embracing the Building Process

- **Stop asking "Why me?" and start asking "What for?"**
    - There is a purpose in every pressure point. Instead of focusing on why things are hard, ask God to reveal what He is building in you through the process.

- **Let God finish what He started.**
    - Don't rush the process. Construction takes time, but the result is glorious. Trust that God is working, even when you don't see the progress.

- **Turn wounds into wisdom.**
    - Every scar has a lesson. Journal what you're learning. Share what you've overcome. Your story will be someone else's survival guide.

- **Celebrate progress over perfection.**
  - Even if you're still in process, you're further than you were yesterday. Celebrate the small victories, because they are building you into who you're meant to be.

Reflection Questions

- **What wounds in your life might God be using to build something new?**
  - Reflect on the areas where you've been wounded. Can you see how God might be using those painful places to shape something beautiful in your life?
- **Have you been resisting breaking or submitting to the process?**
  - Are you fighting against the pain and hardship, or are you allowing God to use it to shape you into something stronger?
- **How is God shaping your character through this season?**
  - Think about the ways your character has been tested and refined in this season. What aspects of your personality or faith are being built through the breaking?

Declaration Prayer

Father, thank You that You do not waste anything—not even my wounds. I choose to trust the breaking, knowing You are building me through it. Strip away what is not like you. Strengthen my character. Stretch my capacity. And let every scar in my life speak of Your healing power. I am not just surviving—I am being shaped. I am not just enduring—I am evolving. In Jesus' name, Amen.

Personal Reflection Space:

"Identify a wound from your past that God is currently using to shape your purpose. How has your perspective changed about this wound?"

NEVER BROKEN

> *"Your life is not falling apart;
> it is being realigned.
> When heaven shakes the earth,
> purpose begins to rise."*

CHAPTER 6

THE SHIFT IN THE SHATTER

Scripture Focus:
"And we know that in all things God works for the good of those who love Him, who have been called according to His purpose."
— Romans 8:28 (NIV)

There is something sacred that happens in the midst of breaking—a divine shift. You may not see it with natural eyes, but in the spirit, it is undeniable. While it may feel like your life is falling apart, like everything is crumbling beyond repair, the truth is this: God is repositioning the pieces. What looks like destruction is often God's strategy for reordering your life according to His perfect will.

We often pray for miracles, yet resist the breaking that births them. We desire the breakthrough but dread the process. But here's a Kingdom revelation: the breaking is not your ending—it's your beginning. It's where heaven steps in and redefines what you thought was over.

God never allows a breaking without the intention to rebuild. And when He rebuilds, it's not just restoration—it's transformation. Stronger. Wiser. More aligned with His purpose than ever before.

So if you find yourself in a season of breaking, don't give in to despair. Lean into the process. Because what feels like shattering is actually the sound of heaven restructuring your destiny.

Before There's a Shift, There's a Shatter

Look at Joseph's story. At seventeen, he dreamed of greatness—visions of his family bowing before him. But the path to that dream wasn't a straight line. Betrayed by his brothers, sold into slavery, falsely accused, and thrown into prison, Joseph endured a series of events that looked like detours and defeats.

But each breaking moment was actually a divine setup. Without betrayal, he wouldn't have ended up in Egypt. Without imprisonment, he wouldn't have met Pharaoh's cupbearer. Without Pharaoh's dream, he wouldn't have been elevated to leadership. God used every shattering moment to shift Joseph from dreamer to deliverer.

In the same way, God is using your breaking points to reposition you. What feels like a setback is often a strategic move. What looks like a detour is divine direction. God is not just comforting you in the crushing—He's calling you forward through it. He's not just patching your pain, He's preparing your purpose.

What the Enemy Meant for Evil...

The enemy rejoices at the sound of a crack, convinced he has finally broken you. But what he doesn't realize is that God has already woven redemption into your story. Joseph understood this when he said in Genesis 50:20, "You intended to harm me, but God intended it for good to accomplish what is now being done, the saving of many lives."

What the enemy meant to destroy you, God uses to develop you. The pain, the betrayal, the rejection, they all become tools in the hands of a Master Potter. They refine your character, sharpen your faith, and deepen your dependence on Him.

And here's the powerful truth: when your faith is tested in the shattering, it becomes trustworthy for the shifting. You're not being broken to be buried, you're being broken to be built.

Shattering Your Structure to Reveal His Strategy

There are moments when God allows the structures we've built—our dreams, goals, and relationships—to shatter. It's not punishment. It's preparation. He lovingly dismantles what we've constructed in our own strength to rebuild something greater, something rooted in His strategy, not ours.

You may have believed your plan was solid. That relationship felt essential. That opportunity looked like the breakthrough you had prayed for. But God sees what we can't. Sometimes, the shatter is the grace of God, clearing space for something far better.

I know this personally.

After years of military service—deployments, leadership, sacrifice—I had my life mapped out. Retire from the Army. Get a stable job. Clock in, clock out. Live a peaceful, quiet life. Amazon seemed perfect: steady income, good benefits, clear promotion path.

Becoming a pastor? That wasn't even on my radar.

If you had told me then that I'd be preaching, leading ministries, and standing in the gap for the broken, I would've laughed. I didn't think I was qualified. I wasn't polished. I didn't feel called.

But God had a different plan—and He wasn't asking for my permission.

When God Shattered My Structure

On paper, everything lined up—interviews, a polished résumé, promising opportunities. But deep inside, I felt restless. Unsettled. Despite everything looking right, it didn't feel right.

Doors that once stood wide open began to slam shut. Interviews that seemed full of potential ended without explanation. Opportunities that looked exciting turned out to be hollow. Every time I tried to push forward, it felt like I was hitting an invisible wall.

Frustrated and confused, I cried out to God, "Why are You blocking what I've worked so hard for?"

Slowly, clarity came. God wasn't punishing me. He was protecting me. Redirecting me.

Mentors began speaking into my life, words I didn't want to hear. Words about leadership. About shepherding. About pastoring. They saw something in me I couldn't yet see: a heart for people. A burden for the broken. A passion for God's Word.

I resisted. I had excuses lined up: "I'm not qualified." "I'm not ready." "I've never been to seminary."

But God isn't concerned with excuses. He's after obedience.

After months of wrestling, I finally surrendered. I gave God my trembling "yes." I laid down my plans and embraced the unknown. I chose His strategy over my structure. And in that surrender, I found peace—not because I had all the answers, but because I knew He did.

Walking in the Shift

Becoming a pastor has stretched me in ways I never imagined. It's tested my pride, my patience, and my perseverance. It's brought me to my knees more times than I can count. Yet it has also filled my life with joy, purpose, and fulfillment deeper than anything I ever thought possible.

I've witnessed marriages restored. I've seen prodigals come home. Souls saved. Chains broken—all because I said "yes" to the shift.

I've baptized men and women who were one decision away from giving up. I've watched altars overflow with people surrendering everything because God used my brokenness to speak life into theirs.

This life, "the one I never asked for," is better than any life I could have built for myself.

God had to break what I thought was important to rebuild what was eternal.

And he'll do the same for you.

When Heaven Interrupts Your Agenda

Divine shifts rarely feel like promotions. They often feel like confusion, disruption, or even chaos. Because shifts don't come packaged in comfort, they come wrapped in surrender.

When God begins to shift your life, it can feel like everything is unraveling. But in the midst of that unraveling, God is weaving a masterpiece.

Mary, the mother of Jesus, understood this. She was planning for marriage, living quietly—until Heaven interrupted. The angel declared, "You will conceive and give birth to a son... the Son of the Most High" (Luke 1:31–32).

In an instant, her world shattered—but her response shifted everything: "Be it unto me according to Your word" (Luke 1:38).

When your life feels shattered, you have two choices: resist the process or surrender to the purpose.

Only surrender leads to transformation.

The Shift Isn't Just for You

Your shift is never just about you. It's about the lives connected to your destiny.

Joseph's shift wasn't for personal power—it was for the preservation of a nation.

David's shift wasn't about wearing a crown—it was to establish the lineage of the Messiah.

Esther's shift wasn't for her comfort—it was to save her people.

Likewise, your shatter and your shift are preparing you to impact others.

Your story will become someone else's survival guide.

Your breakthrough will be someone else's blueprint.

Recognizing the Shift in Real Time

Often, we only recognize the shift looking back. But with spiritual sensitivity, we can discern the signs in real time.

Here are indicators you're in a divine shift:

- **Doors close unexpectedly.** What once seemed sure now vanishes. God is clearing distractions.
- **Relationships change.** People who once "fit" your life may drift away, making room for new alignments.
- **Passions fade; new burdens rise.** What once thrilled you now feels empty. New dreams begin stirring.
- **Comfort zones collapse.** Places you once thrived in now feel foreign. Growth requires new ground.
- **Hidden idols are exposed.** Things you clung to lose their grip. God purifies your heart for His purposes.

These are not signs of failure; they are signs of transition. The shatter is not your downfall—it is your evolution.

Trust the Shift

Friend, the shift may hurt, but it will heal. The shatter may grieve you, but it will grow you.

The breaking may scare you, but it is setting you free. You are not being broken down; you are being built up. You are not being abandoned; you are being advanced.

God is not trying to destroy you—He is preparing you for greater. Trust the shatter. Embrace the shift. Let God transform your breaking into your building.

Because on the other side of the shatter is your shift—and on the other side of your shift is your destiny.

A mentor once told me that divine interruptions are the midwives of destiny. The shattering is not sabotage—it is strategy. God will shake your structure to expose His sovereignty.

Every shift begins with surrender. The shatter is simply the evidence that the old has expired and the new is emerging.

Kingdom Keys

- **Stop cursing what God is using to reposition you.**
  - Just because it's painful doesn't mean it's punishment. Embrace the process instead of resisting it.

- **Surrender your timeline for His divine timing.**
  - God is not late—He's setting the stage for your breakthrough. Trust His timing, even when it doesn't make sense.

- **Refuse to go back to what broke you.**
  - The shift requires you to leave familiar places for faith-filled ones. Don't go back to what God is trying to pull you out of.

Reflection Questions

- **What in your life has recently shattered?**
  - Reflect on what has been broken in your life. How can you see God's hand in the midst of the brokenness?

- **Can you identify any hidden shifts God may be initiating through your pain?**
  - Are there signs that God is positioning you for something greater? How can you recognize these shifts in real time?

- **What would it look like to surrender to the shift rather than resist it?**
  - Think about how you can embrace the changes in your life and trust God's reordering instead of trying to control the process.

Declaration Prayer

Father, I thank You for the shatter—for in it, You are shifting me. I may not understand the breaking, but I trust Your hands. Use every fragment of my life to form something greater than I imagined. I surrender my plans, my timing, and my expectations. Shift me according to Your will. I declare that what felt like loss is leading me to legacy. I am not broken—I'm being positioned. In Jesus' name, Amen.

Personal Reflection Space:

Identify a current storm or shift you are facing. Write down one bold step you can take this week that will actively demonstrate your trust in God's anchors. Commit to taking this action and journal about the changes you observe in yourself and your circumstances as you live out this trust.

_____

_____

_____

> *"You don't need more hustle. You need more alignment. Favor follows function in the Kingdom."*

CHAPTER 7

WALKING IN DIVINE ALIGNMENT

Scripture Focus:
"Trust in the Lord with all your heart and lean not on your own understanding; in all your ways submit to Him, and He will make your paths straight."
— Proverbs 3:5–6 (NIV)

Every believer comes to a pivotal crossroads: Will I follow my own understanding, or will I surrender to the path God has already prepared?

It's not just about staying busy for God—it's about being aligned with Him. When you align with His will, you step into a flow of grace, favor, and divine ease. Not because life is free from obstacles, but because your heart is submitted to His wisdom.

You can be talented and still out of alignment. You can be anointed and still out of order. But when you walk in divine alignment, heaven backs your every step.

Alignment is where purpose meets power. And it is in alignment that you access everything God has ordained for your life.

God's Plan Was in Place Before Your Pain

It's important to remember: you are not an afterthought in the mind of God. You were created with intention, designed with purpose. Psalm 139:16 tells us that all the days ordained for you were written in God's book before one of them came to be. That means your purpose didn't begin with your pain—it preceded it.

Before the betrayal, the rejection, or the disappointment ever showed up in your story, God had already authored your destiny.

The enemy doesn't attack you because of where you are—he attacks you because of where you're going. His goal is to pull you out of alignment with God's plan. But when your steps remain aligned with God's purpose, the enemy's attacks lose their power. You are walking a path that cannot be shaken.

Every struggle, every delay, every detour is not meant to destroy you. It's designed by God to refine your faith and position you closer to the purpose He planned before time began.

Alignment Requires Surrender

Divine alignment doesn't happen by accident. It requires intentional submission. God's will often asks you to lay down your agenda, your desires, and your carefully crafted plans in order to embrace His. The hard truth is this: God's will will cost you yours.

Even Jesus faced this reality in Gethsemane. He prayed, "Father, if You are willing, take this cup from me; yet not my will, but Yours be done" (Luke 22:42). In that moment, Jesus aligned Himself fully with the Father's plan, despite the pain it would bring.

Alignment isn't always comfortable, but it is always crucial. You can either control the outcome or you can trust the One who authored it, but you cannot do both. To walk in alignment is to walk in surrender. It is trusting that God's plan is better, His ways are higher, and His timing is perfect.

When Good Ideas Clash with God Ideas

Just because something looks good doesn't mean it's God's best for you. Many chase good opportunities and miss divine assignments in the process. Saul looked like the ideal king—tall, strong, impressive. But despite his outward appeal, he lacked alignment with God's heart. Meanwhile, David—hidden in the fields, overlooked and ordinary—was chosen because his heart was aligned with God's.

We must be careful not to elevate ambition over obedience. The world celebrates hustle, movement, and outward success, but heaven celebrates alignment in the Kingdom, where you are matters far less than whether God sent you there. Never confuse momentum with mission.

When you're aligned with God's purpose, you won't have to strive or force outcomes—things fall into place by divine design.

The Power of Saying Yes to His Way

Divine alignment begins with a simple yes, not just spoken, but lived. It's a surrender that shows up in your decisions, your relationships, and in how you steward your time, talents, and resources.

When you're aligned with God, doors open that no one can shut. You don't have to manipulate outcomes or chase opportunities. You simply walk in trust, and God directs your steps. Proverbs 3:6 says, "In all your ways submit to Him." Not in some ways, not just on Sundays, but in all your ways. Your business, your marriage, your ministry, your mindset—every part of your life must come under His authority.

Alignment is not partial; it is total. When you fully surrender every area of your life to God, His guidance becomes clear, and His favor begins to flow in ways you could never manufacture on your own.

Signs You're Out of Alignment

God's grace is always present to cover us, but His peace confirms when we are in step with Him. Here are some signs that you may be out of alignment:

- **Constant confusion or double-mindedness**: When you feel pulled in many directions without peace, it's a sign that your will may not be aligned with God's.
- **Fruitless busyness without fulfillment**: You might be working hard, but feeling like you're getting nowhere because your efforts aren't aligned with God's purpose.
- **Doors that once opened now close**: Opportunities that seemed to be blessings might start slipping away. This could be a redirection from God, asking you to realign.
- **Lack of peace, even when things seem successful**: You may achieve success, but if there's no peace, something is out of alignment.
- **Repeating cycles of delay and discouragement**: If you feel stuck in a cycle of frustration, God may be calling you to align with His plan in order to break through.

These are not always punishments—they are often divine alerts. God loves you enough to disturb your comfort so He can redirect your course. If you're experiencing these signs, take time to pause and ask God to reveal where you've veered off track.

Divine Alignment and Divine Acceleration

When you align with God's plan, you don't have to chase what's yours—it will find you. God doesn't bless striving; He blesses obedience. Divine alignment often produces divine acceleration.

Consider the story of Joseph: in one moment, he went from being a prisoner to ruling in the palace. Ruth went from gleaning in a field to becoming Boaz's bride in a single day. Esther stepped into the palace and shifted the fate of a nation.

Why? Because they aligned with the assignment God had for them. They didn't force the doors open; they walked through the one God had opened. When you walk in divine alignment, the doors of opportunity swing wide open, and God's favor follows your every step.

When your heart is yielded and your steps are ordered, you don't have to strive for success. It will find you.

Which reminds me of a leader I had the pleasure of meeting named Terrence. He had been leading worship since he was 16. He was talented, charismatic, and popular—but increasingly empty. The music no longer stirred his spirit. He was performing, not worshiping.

One night, after leading thousands at a conference, he cried alone in the greenroom. He told God, "If You're not in this, I don't want it anymore."

He took three months off and immersed himself in Scripture and stillness. During that time, he felt the Lord say, "I never asked for your gift—I asked for your heart."

He returned to the stage with a different posture: not as a performer, but as a son. Alignment shifted his anointing. People didn't just hear songs—they encountered Presence.

Might I remind you that God is not obligated to bless what He didn't birth. Divine order brings divine overflow. When your will is submitted to His way, your steps are backed by the authority of heaven. Purpose doesn't require effort—it requires obedience.

Kingdom Keys

- **Be willing to pause and pivot.**
  - Sometimes alignment requires stopping what you want to do and recalibrating your course. Trust that God's timing is perfect.
- **Stay sensitive to the Holy Spirit.**
  - The Holy Spirit will nudge you when you start to veer off course. Listen to His gentle guidance.
- **Surround yourself with wise, godly counsel.**
  - People who are aligned with God will help you stay on course and provide wisdom for the journey.

Reflection Questions

- **What areas of your life feel out of sync with God's peace and direction?**
  - Reflect on the areas where you've been striving or feeling unrest. Are there areas where God is calling you to realign?
- **Are there good things you're pursuing that may not be God's things?**
  - Are you chasing opportunities that look good on the surface but might not be part of God's plan for you?
- **What would complete surrender look like for you in this season?**
  - Consider what areas of your life still need to be fully surrendered to God. How can you submit these areas to His will?

Declaration Prayer

Father, I submit my life to Your plan. I surrender my ideas, ambitions, and timelines. Align me with Your will, Your ways, and Your Word. Where I've leaned on my own understanding, correct me. Where I've rushed ahead of you, slow me down. And where I've lagged behind, push me forward. I trust that your path leads to my purpose. Let my steps be ordered, and my heart be anchored in You. In Jesus' name, Amen.

Personal Reflection Space:

Audit your life: Look at your schedule, your relationships, and your habits. What's out of alignment with God's Word? Choose one thing to adjust this week.

> "The enemy tried to bury you.
> God turned it into evidence.
> Your scars are not your story—
> they are your sermon."

CHAPTER 8

∞

SCARS THAT SPEAK

Key Verse:
"By His wounds we are healed."
— Isaiah 53:5

Scars. We all carry them. Some are visible, etched on our skin as reminders of physical pain. Others run deeper, hidden beneath the surface—emotional wounds, spiritual bruises, memories that linger long after the moment has passed. We often try to hide these scars, to cover them up, to pretend they aren't there. We carry shame, believing they're signs of weakness, failure, or disqualification.

But in the Kingdom of God, scars are not shameful—they are sacred. They are not symbols of defeat, but of survival. Scars tell the story of resilience, of endurance, of transformation. They don't prove you were broken—they prove you were healed. You went through the fire and came out refined. You were wounded, but you survived. Cut, but not crushed.

In this chapter, we are going to redefine what it means to carry scars. You'll discover that your pain doesn't disqualify you—it qualifies you. Your scars are your testimony. They speak of battles fought and grace received. They carry a message, one that others need to hear. And when you share that message, your scars become someone else's healing.

Why Your Pain Has a Voice Someone Else Needs to Hear

Pain is universal. We all feel it, though it may come through different doors. Betrayal, loss, rejection, unmet expectations. No one escapes it. And while our stories differ, pain connects us in a deeply human way.

I remember walking through one of the darkest seasons of my life. I had been rejected in a way I never expected, and it shook me to my core. I questioned everything—my value, my purpose, my identity. The weight of it all felt too heavy to share. I thought, Who would care? Who would want to hear about this mess?

Then one day, I listened to someone else share their story. They spoke honestly about their wounds, about how Christ had met them in their brokenness and brought healing. And in their rawness, something ignited in me. Their scars made space for my healing. Their vulnerability gave me the courage to be honest about my own pain. That moment marked a turning point. It reminded me that stories carry power—and pain, when shared, can become a pathway to hope.

Your pain has a voice. It has a purpose. It may feel personal, but it was never meant to be private. When you share your scars—when you let your story speak—you create space for someone else to find healing. Your testimony isn't just about what God did for you. It's about what He wants to do through you.

When we hide our scars, we hide the evidence of God's redemptive power. We silence the very thing that could inspire someone to keep going. Don't let your scars stay silent. Let them speak. Your story may be the key that unlocks someone else's breakthrough.

Moving from Silence to Significance

For many of us, the idea of sharing our scars is terrifying. We fear judgment. We fear being misunderstood. We fear that vulnerability will make us look weak or unworthy. But the truth is, silence is often the enemy of healing. The longer we hide our pain, the more power it holds over us. When we stay quiet, we allow our scars to define us in ways they were never meant to.

When I first began to understand the power of sharing my scars, I was surprised by how freeing it felt. I wasn't just recounting my past, I was reclaiming it. Speaking my story out loud helped me see my journey not as something to be ashamed of, but as something God had used to shape me. The very thing that once threatened to destroy me became a testament to my endurance. I was still here. I had made it through.

Moving from silence to significance means giving your scars a place in your story—not as evidence of defeat, but as proof of grace. Your scars don't define you, but they are part of your becoming. They're not marks of shame—they're marks of survival. They are reminders that you've been through something hard, and by God's grace, you're still standing.

There is something powerful in saying, "This is who I am. This is my story. These are my scars—and I'm not hiding them." That kind of honesty carries weight. It creates a connection. It opens doors for healing. Because your scars don't isolate you—they make you relatable. They make you real. And they become a bridge for others to find hope through your journey.

Learning to Wear Your Scars as a Badge of Grace, Not Guilt

The world may tell you that scars are something to be ashamed of, that you should hide your past, cover your wounds, and present a polished, perfect version of yourself. But in the Kingdom, scars are not signs of failure—they are signs of grace.

Jesus Himself bore scars. His body, broken and beaten, carried the ultimate evidence of God's love and redemption. And those scars? They weren't hidden. They weren't erased. They were shown to Thomas by the disciples as proof of victory over death, sin, and shame.

In the same way, your scars aren't meant to be concealed. They're meant to be seen. They don't expose weakness; they reveal God's strength at work in you.

I once believed my scars, both emotional and physical, made me less than whole. I thought if I could just bury them deep enough, maybe they'd go away. But the more I hid them, the more power they held over me. True freedom came only when I began to wear them as badges of grace. I realized the very things I thought disqualified me were the exact things God was using to qualify me for His purpose.

Every scar tells a story. A battle fought. A valley walked. A wound that healed. They're not symbols of defeat; they're testimonies of survival, resilience, and transformation. They declare, "I went through it—but I didn't stay there. I'm still standing."

And the same is true for you. Your scars mean you're still here. You've endured. You've overcome. And because you're still here, you have something sacred to offer. You carry a testimony someone else desperately needs.

Your scars are not your shame; they are your sermon. They do not define your worth; they reveal God's grace. You may have been broken, but you were never abandoned. You are being made whole, piece by piece. And every scar is a reminder that God is still writing your story.

The Power of Scars: Transforming Pain into Purpose

Pain is never wasted in the Kingdom of God. The very things that once threatened to break you are the things God will use to shape you into who He's called you to be. Your scars are proof of that.

I've learned that when I embrace my scars, I don't just find healing—I find purpose. There is a profound strength that comes from acknowledging the pain you've endured and realizing that God is using it for something greater. Your scars become a platform. A voice. A bridge to someone else's breakthrough. They connect you to those who need your story, those who need to know they, too, can make it through.

When we look at our scars, we often see the pain, the struggle, the fight. But when God looks at our scars, He sees the victory. He sees the testimony. He sees the undeniable evidence of His healing, redemptive power.

So I want to challenge you: Don't hide your scars. Don't let the enemy whisper that your past disqualifies you. Don't let shame silence the story God wants to tell through you. Instead, let your scars speak. Let them testify that God's power is greater than your deepest pain. Let them proclaim that, no matter how fierce the battle, you are still standing by grace, in strength, and with purpose.

Scars as a Testimony to the World

The world needs to see your scars. There are people who need to hear your story because it may be the very thing that gives them hope. Your scars are not a sign that you're finished; they are the testimony that God is not. They're proof that the enemy's attempts to destroy you weren't enough. They're evidence that grace still chooses, mercy still restores, and purpose still prevails.

Take Naomi, for example. She survived years of emotional and physical abuse in a marriage she stayed in "for the kids." When she finally escaped, she was left with guilt, shame, and the haunting question: Could God still use someone like me?

She joined a church recovery group and began, piece by piece, to share her story. One night, after a session, another woman quietly approached her and whispered, "Your story saved my life." That moment changed everything. Today, Naomi leads workshops for women overcoming domestic violence. The very journey that once silenced her has become a road to healing for others.

"Her scarred past now speaks volumes of God's restoring power."

Reflection Questions

- **What scars in your life have you been hiding or trying to cover up?**
    - Consider the scars that you've been ashamed of. What would it look like to embrace them as part of your journey?

- **How can you use your scars as a testimony to others?**
    - Think about how sharing your story can bring healing to someone else. What part of your experience can you share with others to help them find hope?

- **What has your pain taught you, and how can you use that lesson to help others?**
    - Reflect on the lessons you've learned through your pain. How can those lessons be used to serve others and point them to Christ?

Declaration Prayer

Father, I thank You for every scar, every wound, every painful moment that has shaped me into who I am today. I acknowledge that my scars are not signs of defeat—they are signs of Your grace at work in me. I choose to wear them as badges of honor, as evidence of your power to heal and restore. I release all shame and guilt associated with my past and embrace the purpose You've ordained for my life. Let my scars speak to the world of Your goodness, and let my story be a testimony of Your unshakable love. In Jesus' name, Amen.

Personal Reflection Space:

Write out then share your testimony, publicly or privately with someone who is struggling. Let your scars speak healing.

"Wholeness is when your history no longer hinders your destiny. You are not being fixed— you are being revealed."

CHAPTER 9

※

BECOMING WHOLE

Scripture Focus:
"Therefore, if anyone is in Christ, the new creation has come:
The old has gone, the new is here!"
— 2 Corinthians 5:17 (NIV)

There comes a moment in every believer's life when something sacred shifts—a revelation that pierces through the noise of pain, confusion, and past disappointments. It's the moment you realize: you were never broken beyond repair. You were being prepared.

What looked like destruction was actually divine construction. What felt like ruin was the start of divine renovation. What seemed like the end was actually the beginning of who you were always meant to become.

You weren't breaking down—you were being built up.

This is the unveiling of purpose, the divine perspective that changes everything. God was never trying to bury you; He was planting you. And now, the old has gone. The news has come. You are not who you were—and that's the beauty of grace. Redefining Brokenness

We must begin with a bold truth: Brokenness in the Kingdom does not equal defeat. In the hands of God, even the shattered becomes sacred. What the world calls "broken," God calls "becoming."

The enemy wants to whisper that you are too far gone, too wounded, too weak to ever be used by God. He wants you to define yourself by your damage, to get stuck in the lie that your brokenness is the end of the story. But God speaks a better word. He says, "You are in process. You are being refined. You are becoming who I created you to be."

The breaking was never meant to be your identity—it was your initiation into something greater. What you've endured is part of your transformation. You are not the sum of your scars. You are the sum of your becoming.

Preparation Always Precedes Purpose

Before David ever wore a crown, he played a harp in the fields. Before Esther entered the palace, she endured loss and displacement. Before Joseph became second in command, he survived betrayal and prison. Their pain wasn't random; it was preparation.

God never wastes pain. Every trial, every setback, every heartbreak has been part of His divine plan to shape you for what's ahead. The rejection, the loneliness, the betrayal, they weren't accidents. They were chiseling your character, deepening your faith, and forging your resilience.

God never skips preparation. Purpose without process leads to collapse. But when you endure the fire, you emerge refined, empowered, and aligned with your calling. The waiting, the breaking, the scars—they are not in vain. They are the very path to your destiny.

You Are the Masterpiece in the Making

Ephesians 2:10 reminds us, "For we are God's masterpiece. He has created us anew in Christ Jesus, so we can do the good things He planned for us long ago."

A masterpiece is never rushed. It's not mass-produced or haphazardly assembled. It's carefully crafted—shaped with intention, refined through pressure, and perfected with time. Becoming who God created you to be is not an overnight transformation; it's a sacred process.

You are not on the assembly line of life—you are in the hands of the Master Artist. Every brushstroke matters. Every season of waiting, every tear cried, every breakthrough fought for is part of His divine design.

You are not just surviving—you are becoming. Day by day, moment by moment, God is shaping you into a vessel that carries His glory and fulfills His purpose. Trust the process. The Artist never wastes His paint.

It Was Never About What You Lost

God isn't just restoring what you lost; He's revealing what you never knew you had. Often, we grieve the things God had to remove, not realizing He's clearing space for something far greater.

Abraham had to leave the land he knew. Ruth had to walk away from Moab. Peter had to drop his nets. What they left behind was nothing compared to what God was calling them into. The same is true for you.

What you thought you lost wasn't meant to stay. God was separating you, not to diminish you, but to elevate you. To refine your focus, deepen your trust, and position you for a higher purpose.

You are not less because of the loss. You are becoming more. Every surrender, every shift, every goodbye is shaping you into the person God has always seen in you: stronger, clearer, and more aligned with your calling.

When You Embrace the Becoming

Everything changes when you realize you're not broken—you're in process. You stop mistaking delays for denials. You stop interpreting God's silence as

His absence. You stop viewing struggle as failure. Instead, you begin to see every moment as part of the masterpiece God is shaping.

This is where joy returns. This is where peace begins to flood your soul. This is where confidence rises—not in your performance, but in His promise.

When you embrace the truth that you're becoming, you stop judging your worth by how far you've fallen and start celebrating how far you've come.

You're not broken—you're evolving. And that evolution is holy.

The Journey from Wounded to Whole

Your scars are not a liability; they're a testimony of what you've survived. Your tears weren't in vain; they watered the seeds of your future. Your waiting wasn't wasted—it was God weaving purpose deep within you.

God uses everything—every misstep, every failure, every broken place. He is the only one who can take shattered pieces and form sacred beauty. When the enemy thought you were finished, God was just getting started. Your story is not one of defeat; it's one of divine redemption.

During one of our men's fellowship gatherings, a young man named Jordan shared his testimony. He was a PK—a pastor's kid, who grew up in church, leading youth groups, memorizing Scripture, doing all the "right" things. But behind the performance, he silently battled porn addiction, depression, and deep identity confusion.

In college, Jordan hit rock bottom. After a suicide attempt, he was hospitalized. There, a nurse prayed over him and whispered, "God isn't angry at you, He's waiting for the real you." That moment marked a turning point.

Jordan began recovery, pursued counseling, and eventually became a licensed counselor himself. Today, he helps young men navigate the hidden battles he once faced. Wholeness, for him, didn't come from perfection—it came from honesty.

He learned that God wasn't after his performance; He was after his heart.

I shared with Jordan that identity transformation is a daily process of renewing the mind. You don't become whole in a single moment—you build the architecture of wholeness through repetition, reflection, and spiritual truth.

Each time you reject a lie and declare God's Word, you're rewiring your mind for truth. The new creation isn't just a spiritual reality—it becomes your mental blueprint, formed by daily practice and divine grace.

Kingdom Truths

- **What you thought disqualified you is the very thing God will use to qualify you.**
    - God's grace takes what the world sees as weak and transforms it into strength.
- **His power is made perfect in your weakness.**
    - It's through your vulnerability that His strength is most visible.
- **Becoming never ends—it's a daily transformation.**
    - From glory to glory, you are being conformed into the image of Christ.

Reflection Questions

- **What have you viewed as "brokenness" that might actually be God's preparation?**
    - Take a moment to reflect on areas where you've been hurt or broken. Could it be that God is using those moments to shape your future?
- **How have you changed for the better because of your past wounds?**
    - Look back on your wounds. How have they transformed you into the person you are today?

- **In what areas do you need to stop striving and start surrendering to God's process?**
  - Are there areas where you've been trying to control the outcome instead of trusting God's timing?

Declaration Prayer

Father, thank You for revealing the truth behind the pain. I am not broken beyond use—I am being prepared for purpose. I release every false label, every lie, every limitation. I choose to see my life through the lens of Heaven. What I thought was breaking me was building me. What I thought was the end was the beginning of my becoming. I trust You, Lord. I surrender to the masterpiece you are shaping in me. I am never broken—just becoming. In Jesus' name, Amen

Personal Reflection Space:

Write a letter to your former self—the broken version of you. Speak life, purpose, and truth into the version that almost gave up.

_____
_____
_____
_____
_____
_____
_____
_____
_____
_____

*"You are not just healed—
you are commissioned. You are
the visible evidence that purpose
prevails over pain."*

CONCLUSION

THE EVIDENCE OF PURPOSE

Key Verse:
"You are a letter from Christ... written not with ink but with the Spirit of the living God."
— 2 Corinthians 3:3

As I reflect on the journey that brought me here, one powerful truth rises above the rest: God doesn't just want you healed; He wants you whole. There's a difference. Healing mends what was broken. But wholeness? Wholeness completes you. It integrates every part of your story—your past, your pain, your process—into something purposeful and powerful.

Wholeness isn't about pretending you were never wounded. It's about allowing the Spirit of God to write redemption across every chapter of your life. It's about stepping into divine alignment where even the broken pieces shine with evidence of His glory. When you are whole, your life reflects the fullness of God's plan—not in theory, but in lived, visible testimony.

God doesn't just want to restore what you lost. He wants to reveal Himself through you. You were never meant to merely survive; you were meant to be a signpost that points others to the power of God's redemptive love, not just when things are easy, but especially in the trials. Especially in the tension. Especially in the places where you once felt disqualified.

You are living evidence that grace still works. That pain can lead to purpose. That is what the enemy tried to destroy, but God can transform it into destiny.

In this chapter, we'll explore what it looks like to live as proof of God's plan. To walk in clarity instead of confusion. To no longer chase healing as a destination, but to embrace wholeness as a way of life. And ultimately, to become the message you once needed—to be the letter someone else is desperate to read.

The Canvas of Your Life: A Letter Written by God

Have you ever paused to consider that your life is a letter from Christ? In 2 Corinthians 3:3, Paul reminds us that we are "letters... written not with ink but with the Spirit of the living God." That means your life is not random. It's not meaningless. It's a living epistle, authored by God Himself.

Every chapter matters. The highs and the lows, the breakthroughs and the breakdowns, the joy and the pain, they are all inked into a greater story of redemption. And the message God is writing through you is not about perfection. It's about transformation. It's not about how flawlessly you've lived, but how faithfully you've been formed.

You may not see the full picture now, but your life is meant to be read by your family, your community, and the world around you. Your scars, your progress, your silent prayers, they are all part of the testimony that God is real, God is present, and God is powerful.

I remember a time when my life felt like a series of missteps; random, painful, and confusing. I couldn't imagine how any of it could have a purpose. But now, looking back, I see how God used every single moment to shape me. Every detour, every delay, every disappointment was part of the story He was writing through me. What once felt like a meaningless struggle is now meaningful evidence of His grace.

This is what it means to live as evidence. To stop waiting until your life is "together" to show up. To stop hiding the messy parts. To allow God to use even the parts you once tried to erase. Your life becomes a message that says, "God is not finished with me—and if He's still writing my story, He's still writing yours too."

So stand boldly in your becoming. Let your life declare, "Here I am, Lord, use me."

The Joy of Becoming the Message You Once Needed to Hear

We've all had moments when we were desperate for something—anything—that could help us make sense of our struggles. Maybe it was a word of encouragement, a voice of wisdom, or simply someone who understood the depth of our pain. We longed for reassurance that we weren't alone and that the story wasn't over.

Here's the beauty of walking in divine purpose: as you heal, as you grow, as you step into your own transformation, you become what you once needed. You become the message someone else is praying for.

I remember sitting in the pews at church, listening to others share how they overcame adversity, how God met them in their darkest places. Their words ignited something in me. I thought, "I want to be that person for someone. I want my life to say that God is faithful, that grace is enough, that no story is too broken to be redeemed."

And friend, you have that same calling. You don't need a polished past or a perfect present to be used by God. Your real story—messy, raw, and full of grace—is exactly what someone else needs. It's your honesty, your endurance, and your transformation that will breathe hope into others.

There is immeasurable joy in becoming the message you once searched for. Not just surviving, but thriving. Not just making it through, but turning around and offering your hand to the next weary soul.

You are no longer waiting for someone to speak into your life. You are the voice now. You are the evidence. You are the living proof that God's redemptive plan works, that grace truly heals, and that no matter how deep the pit, purpose still prevails.

Living as Evidence of God's Redemptive Plan

To live as evidence of God's redemptive plan is to embrace the truth that your life carries a higher purpose. It's not about avoiding struggle or pretending things are perfect. It's about recognizing that, in every season—whether bright or broken—God is working. He is redeeming your moments, your pain, and even your missteps for His glory.

I've lived through seasons where I couldn't see what God was doing. Times when I felt lost, confused, or even forgotten. I wrestled with questions, frustrations, and silent prayers that seemed to go unanswered. But looking back, it was in those very moments of uncertainty that my faith deepened. It was in wrestling that I discovered the roots of trust. I began to see how every thread of pain, every knot of failure, every tear shed was being woven into a masterpiece I couldn't yet comprehend.

God wastes nothing. Not your brokenness, not your delays, not even your doubts. He is present in your process; actively shaping, refining, and aligning your story with His divine purpose.

When we shift our focus from the discomfort of now to the bigger picture of what God is building, we begin to realize something profound: every chapter of our story matters. The seasons that feel like detours are often the ones carrying the greatest growth.

You are living proof that God's plan is unfolding, even in real time. And though you may not see the full picture today, one day, you'll look back and realize He was writing beauty into every single line. Your story isn't finished, and the Author is still holding the pen.

Embracing a Future Fueled by Clarity, Not Confusion

Living as evidence of God's redemptive plan also means choosing clarity over confusion. In seasons of struggle, it's easy to lose sight of the bigger picture. The fog of uncertainty settles in, clouding our vision and making it hard to understand the purpose behind the pain. But this is where faith steps in.

When we align our hearts with God's purpose, He gives us clarity—not always in the form of complete answers, but in the form of peace. It's the kind of clarity that doesn't always eliminate doubt but quiets it. The kind that whispers, "I'm still working, even when you can't see how."

This clarity isn't something we earn by striving. It comes through surrender. It's found in trusting that God is both the Author and the Finisher of our story. When we release our grip on the need to control, we begin to walk in the assurance that He is guiding us, even through the fog.

I've walked through seasons where everything felt like a blur. Where the future seemed more like a question mark than a promise. And yet, God gave me just enough light to take the next step. That's all I needed. One step at a time, He led me—faithfully, patiently, purposefully. And now, looking back, I can see how every step, even the uncertain ones, was part of His divine design.

Becoming the Evidence of Purpose

You are not just a product of your circumstances—you are the evidence that God's purpose is still alive, still active, and still unfolding today. Your life is a living, breathing testimony that grace still chooses, mercy still restores, and destiny cannot be denied.

Living as evidence of purpose means recognizing that your story matters. It means embracing the power of your testimony. Every step, every heartbreak, every healing, every moment of waiting, every season of becoming—declares the faithfulness of a God who never abandons His plans. Even the painful moments have been part of something beautiful.

You are not a victim of your past. You are a vessel of redemption. Your life is the proof that God takes what was meant to destroy you and transforms it into something greater than you could've imagined. You are becoming the evidence that God still works miracles, still restores, and still calls His people into divine purpose.

You've come a long way.

From pain to purpose.

From confusion to clarity.

From fragments to fullness.

From "Why me?" to "Use me."

If there's one truth I want etched into your spirit as you close this book, it's this: You were never broken, you were being built.

I've seen it in my own life. From moments of personal struggle to seasons of loss, I've questioned the purpose of it all. But looking back, I see that every experience—every tear, every valley, every setback—was part of God's blueprint. I wasn't falling apart. I was being reassembled in ways I couldn't have imagined. The pain wasn't the end; it was the shaping ground for purpose.

Everything the enemy meant for evil, God used for your becoming. I know it's hard to see in the middle of it. The valley feels endless. The pressure was unbearable. The tears were unrelenting. But it's in those hidden, lonely places—where no one sees your struggle, that God does His deepest work.

Those are the places where foundations are laid, where character is forged, and where calling is clarified.

He's been faithful—not just in the public victories, but in the private battles. Not just when you stood tall, but when you could barely crawl. Not just in answered prayers, but in silent nights filled with questions. In all of it, He was there.

You are not a product of your pain. You are the evidence of God's purpose.

I know this personally. As a young man, I believed the lie that I was too broken to be used by God. Growing up surrounded by poverty, loss, and uncertainty made me feel like I was doomed to fail. I let my setbacks define me. But now, I see clearly: those struggles didn't disqualify me, they prepared me. Every loss, every failure, every hard lesson was part of the process that revealed my purpose.

Your story matters. Your scars hold wisdom. Your life declares to the world that grace still chooses, mercy still restores, and purpose still prevails.

Live as a Message

The world doesn't need more perfect people. It needs real people, people who've walked through the fire and didn't lose their faith. People who can say, "I've been through the breaking, but I didn't break. I've been crushed, but not consumed. I've been struck down, but not destroyed" (see 2 Corinthians 4:8–9).

What the world needs is your story, not the polished version that hides the pain, not the curated narrative shaped to meet expectations. The world needs the raw, unfiltered truth—the version where you fought through dark nights and still held on. The version where you wrestled with doubt but refused to let go of hope. That's where the power is. That's what reaches people.

Your scars, your struggles, your battles, they don't disqualify you. They are what make you real. And your realness is what connects with the brokenhearted, the weary, and the ones who are barely holding on. They don't need your perfection. They need your authenticity. They need to know redemption is possible.

I think back to the darkest moments in my own life, times when I couldn't imagine anything good coming from the pain I was in. I never dreamed those breaking points would become the foundation of my purpose. I didn't see myself as a pastor, a leader, or an author. But God did. He saw every shattered piece and already knew how to arrange them into something whole, something beautiful, something useful.

Your life is the message. Your journey is the sermon. And the message is this: God uses broken things to birth beautiful things.

Your life is living proof that no pain is wasted. Your journey is evidence that what the enemy meant for evil, God can and will turn for good. What once tried to destroy you is now shaping your destiny.

You've made it through—and now, you carry the testimony that grace still chooses, mercy still restores, and purpose still prevails.

What's Next?

Now it's time to walk it out. This is where transformation takes root—not just in what you believe, but in how you live.

Keep becoming.

Keep surrendering.

Keep trusting the process.

Keep pointing people to the One who brought you through.

There is no finish line in the journey of becoming. Every day is another step into growth, another opportunity to evolve, another chance to walk in the fullness of your purpose. Your brokenness doesn't define you; it shapes you. It's the evidence that God is molding you into who you were always meant to be.

And as you move forward, remember: God isn't just focused on the destination—He's present in every step. He's working on you, in you, and through you, even in the middle of the process.

Let this be the season where you stop hiding the broken pieces—and start letting God use them. Someone out there is waiting for your story. Someone needs to see what redemption looks like. Someone needs permission to believe again, because of you.

Your testimony isn't just for your healing. It's for theirs, too.

You didn't make it this far just to survive. You made it to testify. To bear witness to the power of God who heals, restores, and redeems. The struggles you've faced, the pain you've carried, the fears you've overcome—they weren't wasted. They were preparing you to lead others to the same freedom.

You are living proof that grace still chooses, mercy still restores, and purpose still prevails.

Final Prayer

Father, thank You for every valley, every lesson, every breakthrough. Thank you that I am not defining me by what happened to me, but by what you are doing in me. Let my life be living evidence of Your goodness. Let my voice echo with Your glory. Let my journey point others to Jesus. I am not broken, I am becoming. And because of you, I will never walk the same again. In Jesus' name, Amen.

As you continue walking through life, let this truth take root deep within your spirit: You are not broken beyond repair. You are in the process of becoming. Every struggle you've faced is a piece of your divine puzzle. Every challenge you've endured is part of the masterpiece God is painting with your life.

You've survived, and now, you shine as living proof that God's grace still works.

So keep walking.

Keep becoming.

Keep shining the light of hope that others are desperate to see.

The world needs your story. And God is still writing it.

A PERSONAL LETTER FROM THE AUTHOR

Dear Reader,

Thank you.

Thank you for opening this book, for turning its pages, and for allowing me to walk with you through the sacred ground of your story. I don't take that lightly. I know what it costs to confront the broken places. I know the courage it takes to peel back the layers, to face the wounds, and to still believe that God is writing something beautiful from it all.

This book wasn't written from a platform—it was written from a place of pain that God met with purpose. And if it has spoken to you, stirred something in you, or helped you see your scars a little differently... then it was worth every tear it took to write.

My prayer is that *Never Broken* wouldn't just inspire you—but activate you. That it would push you beyond survival and into surrender. That it would awaken the warrior inside you—the one God has been shaping in the shadows.

God has not wasted a single moment of your journey. He is the Master Builder, and even the rubble in your life holds resurrection power in His hands. So keep going. Keep healing. Keep becoming. You don't have to have it all together to walk in purpose—you just have to be willing.

As you step forward from these pages, know this: You are seen. You are loved. You are chosen.

And I'm cheering you on, every step of the way.

With honor and hope,
Sylvester

PASS IT ON

If this book has spoken to you—if it reminded you that you're not too far gone, too broken, or too far behind—then know this: someone in your life needs that same reminder. Somebody you know is drowning in silence, smiling in public, but dying inside. They don't need another church cliché. They need **you**.

Would you consider passing this message along?

Share this book with someone you know who is walking through the fire. Someone questioning their worth, hiding their scars, or silently asking, *"Can God still use me?"* Let them know that the answer is "Yes". Let this story become part of *their* restoration journey, too.

And if this message blessed you, I'd be honored if you'd take a moment to leave a review. Your words could be the very thing that gives another reader the courage to take the first step into their own becoming.

You've read the pages.

You've wrestled with the questions.

You've begun the journey.

Now be the reason someone else believes they can begin again.

Because purpose is never meant to stay in one set of hands—it multiplies when it's shared.

ABOUT THE AUTHOR

Sylvester Jenkins III is a passionate communicator, pastor, and purpose-driven leader dedicated to helping people rise from brokenness into divine purpose. As an Army veteran, community leader, and Discipleship Pastor, he combines real-world experience with biblical insight to empower individuals to live fully aligned with God's plan.

With a heart for transformation and a message rooted in grace, Sylvester draws from his own journey through pain, identity, and restoration. His story is proof that God doesn't just heal wounds—He uses them to shape warriors.

Whether preaching from a pulpit, mentoring future leaders, or writing transformational content, Sylvester's mission is clear: to awaken purpose, restore hope, and remind people that in the hands of God, nothing is ever wasted.

You can connect with him through his website or follow him on social media, and his leadership journey online at www.sylvesterjenkinsiii.com.

SMALL GROUP DISCUSSION GUIDE

A 9-Week Journey Toward Healing, Wholeness, and Purpose

This guide is designed to help your group engage with the powerful truths in *Never Broken*, creating space for honest conversations, deeper faith, and meaningful transformation. Each week includes a theme focus, key scripture, discussion questions, and a suggested group activity or prayer challenge.

Week 1 – The Breaking Point

Theme: Recognizing rock-bottom moments as the beginning of restoration
Scripture: John 12:24
Discussion Questions:

- What does "breaking point" look like in your life story?
- How do you usually respond to pain—withdrawal, distraction, or control?

Group Activity: Invite each member to write down an area they've been avoiding and surrender it in prayer together.

Week 2 – Beauty from the Ashes

Theme: Letting go of false identities and receiving God's restoration
Scripture: Isaiah 61:3
Discussion Questions:

- What ashes have you been clinging to?
- How do cultural or personal lies about pain shape how you see yourself?
  Group Activity: Burn or tear up symbolic "false labels" and replace them with spoken truths over each other.

Week 3 – When the Mask Falls Off

Theme: Choosing vulnerability and authenticity over image
Scripture: 2 Corinthians 3:18
Discussion Questions:

- What mask have you been wearing to protect yourself?
- How can vulnerability become a form of worship in your life?
  Group Activity: Journal a raw, honest prayer, then read Psalm 139 together.

Week 4 – Carried Through the Cracks

Theme: Embracing God's sustaining grace in weakness
Scripture: Psalm 34:18
Discussion Questions:

- What cracks are showing up in your strength lately?
- What would it look like to let God carry you instead of holding it all together?
  Group Activity: Group encouragement circle—each person speaks one word of life over the person to their left.

Week 5 – Living Whole

Theme: Walking in the fruit of healing
Scripture: John 10:10

Discussion Questions:
- What visible changes have you seen in your life since beginning to heal?
- How does emotional maturity connect to your spiritual growth?
  Group Activity: Accountability partners—commit to checking in weekly on one discipline of wholeness.

Week 6 – The Shift in the Shatter

Theme: Trusting God's redirection through disruption
Scripture: Romans 8:28
Discussion Questions:
- What recent shift in your life might actually be divine redirection?
- How do you tend to respond when your plans fall apart?
  Group Activity: Create a "Shift Testimony" wall with sticky notes—what God is shifting in each person's life.

Week 7 – Walking in Divine Alignment

Theme: Submitting your steps to God's perfect will
Scripture: Proverbs 3:5–6
Discussion Questions:
- Where in your life are you leaning on your own understanding?
- What does complete surrender look like for you right now?
  Group Activity: Map your personal alignment journey (timeline style) and pray over future direction.

Week 8 – Scars That Speak

Theme: Using your testimony as a healing tool for others
Scripture: Isaiah 53:5
Discussion Questions:
- What scar are you afraid to share—and why?
- How might God use your story to bring hope to someone else?

Group Activity: Testimony circle—each person shares one story of survival and God's grace.

Week 9 – Becoming Whole

Theme: Embracing identity and purpose in the process
Scripture: 2 Corinthians 5:17
Discussion Questions:
- How do you see yourself differently now than at the beginning of this study?
- What does "becoming" mean to you today?
  Group Activity: Write a letter to your former self. Seal it. Optional: share it with the group or read it privately.

www.ingramcontent.com/pod-product-compliance
Lightning Source LLC
Chambersburg PA
CBHW072012290426
44109CB00018B/2216